Endgame for the West in Afghanistan? Explaining the Decline in Support for the War in Afghanistan in the United States, Great Britain, Canada, Australia, France and Germany

Charles A. Miller

This is a curated and comprehensive collection of the most important works covering matters related to national security, diplomacy, defense, war, strategy, and tactics. The collection spans centuries of thought and experience, and includes the latest analysis of international threats, both conventional and asymmetric. It also includes riveting first person accounts of historic battles and wars.

Some of the books in this Series are reproductions of historical works preserved by some of the leading libraries in the world. As with any reproduction of a historical artifact, some of these books contain missing or blurred pages, poor pictures, errant marks, etc. We believe these books are essential to this collection and the study of war, and have therefore brought them back into print, despite these imperfections.

We hope you enjoy the unmatched breadth and depth of this collection, from the historical to the just-published works.

The
Letort Papers

In the early 18th century, James Letort, an explorer and fur trader, was instrumental in opening up the Cumberland Valley to settlement. By 1752, there was a garrison on Letort Creek at what is today Carlisle Barracks, Pennsylvania. In those days, Carlisle Barracks lay at the western edge of the American colonies. It was a bastion for the protection of settlers and a departure point for further exploration. Today, as was the case over two centuries ago, Carlisle Barracks, as the home of the U.S. Army War College, is a place of transition and transformation.

In the same spirit of bold curiosity that compelled the men and women who, like Letort, settled the American west, the Strategic Studies Institute (SSI) presents *The Letort Papers*. This series allows SSI to publish papers, retrospectives, speeches, or essays of interest to the defense academic community which may not correspond with our mainstream policy-oriented publications.

If you think you may have a subject amenable to publication in our *Letort Paper* series, or if you wish to comment on a particular paper, please contact Dr. Antulio J. Echevarria II, Director of Research, U.S. Army War College, Strategic Studies Institute, 122 Forbes Ave, Carlisle, PA 17013-5244. The phone number is (717) 245-4058; e-mail address is *antulio.echevarria@us.army.mil*. We look forward to hearing from you.

ENDGAME FOR THE WEST IN AFGHANISTAN? EXPLAINING THE DECLINE IN SUPPORT FOR THE WAR IN AFGHANISTAN IN THE UNITED STATES, GREAT BRITAIN, CANADA, AUSTRALIA, FRANCE AND GERMANY

Charles A. Miller

June 2010

The views expressed in this report are those of the author and do not necessarily reflect the official policy or position of the Department of the Army, the Department of Defense, or the U.S. Government. Authors of Strategic Studies Institute (SSI) publications enjoy full academic freedom, provided they do not disclose classified information, jeopardize operations security, or misrepresent official U.S. policy. Such academic freedom empowers them to offer new and sometimes controversial perspectives in the interest of furthering debate on key issues. This report is cleared for public release; distribution is unlimited.

*****

*****

Comments pertaining to this report are invited and should be forwarded to: Director, Strategic Studies Institute, U.S. Army War College, 122 Forbes Ave, Carlisle, PA 17013-5244.

*****

The author would like to thank the following individuals who have helped with the *Endgame for the West in Afghanistan:* Professors Peter Feaver and Chris Gelpi of Duke University, Professor Janice Stein of the University of Toronto, and Professor Christopher Dandeker of King's College, London.

*****

All Strategic Studies Institute (SSI) publications may be downloaded free of charge from the SSI website. Hard copies of this report may also be obtained free of charge by placing an order on the SSI website. The SSI website address is: *www.StrategicStudiesInstitute.army.mil.*

*****

The Strategic Studies Institute publishes a monthly e-mail newsletter to update the national security community on the research of our analysts, recent and forthcoming publications, and upcoming conferences sponsored by the Institute. Each newsletter also provides a strategic commentary by one of our research analysts. If you are interested in receiving this newsletter, please subscribe on the SSI website at *www.StrategicStudiesInstitute.army.mil/newsletter/.*

ISBN 1-58487-447-3

FOREWORD

This piece was mostly written over the summer of 2009, with some modifications designed to take into account the initial reaction to President Barack Obama's announcement of a new strategy for Afghanistan in the winter of that year. However, more time will be required to gauge the true effect of the new strategy and the rhetorical campaign accompanying it. Readers should seek to use this work to investigate the linkages between various theories of public opinion and foreign policy with respect to the war in Afghanistan up to and including August 2009.

DOUGLAS C. LOVELACE, JR.
Director
Strategic Studies Institute

ABOUT THE AUTHOR

CHARLES A. MILLER worked for a number of years in the business world in companies such as Coors Brewing Company and Barclays Wealth Management. In 2008 he joined the Political Science Department at Duke University as a Ph.D. student. Mr. Miller holds a B.A. in modern languages from the University of Cambridge and an M.A. in international relations from the University of Chicago.

SUMMARY

Domestic support for the war is often mentioned as one of the key battlegrounds of the Afghan conflict. A variety of explanations have been put forward in the media and in the political realm to explain why this war, which once commanded overwhelming popular support in almost all participating countries, is now opposed by a majority, even in the United States itself. Casualties, lack of equitable multilateral burden sharing, confused and shifting rationales on the part of the political leadership for the war and a "contagion" effect from the unpopularity of the Iraq war have all been cited at one time or another.

This monograph contends that while most of these factors have played a role to some extent, the main reason why the Afghan war has lost support among the public of the main participating countries is the combination of mounting casualties along with the increasing perception that the effort on the ground is failing. This conclusion is drawn from in-depth case studies of the United States and five of its key allies—the United Kingdom (UK), France, Germany, Canada, and Australia. These countries include the top three troop contributing nations to the Allied effort in Afghanistan (the United States, the UK, and Germany), and the three who have suffered the heaviest casualties (the United States, the UK, and Canada). Moreover, these nations vary greatly in terms of their pre-September 11, 2001 (9/11) relations with the United States, historical tradition of, and public tolerance towards the use of force overseas, level of commitment to the Afghan war, and rhetorical strategies chosen by their political leadership to justify the deployment to their peoples. The fact that a common thread—domestic support falls as the course of the war deteriorates—is still discernible is remarkable in light of the diversity of the cases studied.

ENDGAME FOR THE WEST IN AFGHANISTAN? EXPLAINING THE DECLINE IN SUPPORT FOR THE WAR IN AFGHANISTAN IN THE UNITED STATES, GREAT BRITAIN, CANADA, AUSTRALIA, FRANCE AND GERMANY

INTRODUCTION

In contrast to the war in Iraq, the war in Afghanistan enjoyed widespread domestic U.S. and international support. Widely perceived in the wake of September 11, 2001 (9/11) as a just and legal war to prevent future terrorist atrocities, the U.S.-led war had the active support of many allies from Europe and elsewhere. However, at the time of writing, this support has dropped off dramatically among the public in all six countries under study. In the United States, support levels as high as 91 percent in early 2002[1] have declined to approximately 50-60 percent in 2008,[2] with many polls showing a majority now opposed to the war.[3] In the United Kingdom (UK), support fell from over 70 percent in early 2002 to just over 30 percent in the summer of 2008.[4] In Canada, previous high support levels of 60-70 percent[5] have been transformed into a current support rate a little above 35 percent.[6] In Australia, the war in Afghanistan, an electoral asset for John Howard's Liberals in the 2001 election,[7] now enjoys minority support of around 42 percent, according to the latest polls.[8] In France, support fell from 67 percent shortly after 9/11[9] to a mere 34 percent[10] by September 2008. Finally, Germany has seen a similar drop in support from a comfortable majority of 61 percent in favor of action[11] to a small minority of 27 percent[12] by December 2009. From a policy perspective, this drop in support is concerning.

As is outlined shortly, the main finding of this monograph is that, although other factors such as confusing and inconsistent rhetoric from political leaders have been important, the key driver of the fall in support for the war in Afghanistan is a combination of casualties with an increasing perception that the war on the ground is being lost. If policymakers wish to halt this decline in public support, the single most important thing they can do is to consistently articulate a clear and credible plan to achieve success in Afghanistan. Other options, such as tightening the rhetorical justification for the war or inducing greater multilateral cooperation, may have some effect at the margins, but if publics do not believe the war can be won, then Afghanistan will be a lost cause in the court of public opinion.

This monograph will address the reasons behind this universal fall in support by looking at each country on a case-by-case basis. While it may be supposed that all of the countries in this monograph share certain generic similarities as highly developed democracies, each public's attitude is also presumed to be shaped by country-specific historical and cultural factors, and by the differing experiences of their militaries in Afghanistan.

Each country will form a separate case study. In turn, each case study will be prefaced with a short outline of the given country's recent historical experience with, and public attitudes towards the U.S. and towards the use of force overseas. Any assertion that a given country is "pacifist-inclined" or "pro-interventionist" must be backed up by historical facts and hard data, because in some cases—for example France or Canada—many stereotypes, which are popular even among well-informed policymakers, turn out on closer inspection to be poorly founded. Along with opinion polls on public attitudes both of the United States and of the use of force in international affairs, this short introductory section will include information on whether the country in question imposes parliamentary caveats on its forces in Afghanistan. Unfortunately, for secrecy reasons, we are not aware of the actual content of most of these caveats. However, the North Atlantic Treaty Organization (NATO) has made public information on which countries do and do not have caveats. This will be used, as it provides a good indication of a given country's preexisting attitudes to the use of force.

In seeking to explain the fall in support in each case, the author draws on both the academic literature on casualty sensitivity developed from the study of public opinion in previous conflicts and on theories that are popular in policy circles and the news media with respect to Afghanistan. The remainder of this introductory section will outline these theories. Academic theories are not important because they hold some kind of intrinsic, aesthetic value but because they provide policymakers with some guidance on where to look for the causes of an important phenomenon such as the decline in support for the war in Afghanistan. Academic debates are ultimately important only in so far as they are capable of yielding actionable and accurate advice to policymakers. At the same time, the academic literature does have some advantages over the news media debate in its ability to clearly and rigorously to spell out the mechanisms by which causes are linked to effects. With some news media-driven theories—such as the theory that the Afghanistan war has contracted illegitimacy from the war in Iraq—the precise way in which this process plays out in the minds of individual voters is somewhat nebulous.

Thus theories that are popular in the news media will sometimes require some additional fleshing out to gauge how crucial they really are.

The first set of explanations popular both in academia and in news media and policy circles is that the decline in public support for the war is a straightforward result of increasing casualties. There are two variants of this "casualty phobia" explanation. First, there is the view that public support for the war starts high but then drops rapidly when the first casualties are sustained, then drops more slowly afterwards—this is known as the "logarithmic casualties" theory and is associated with John Mueller.[13] Second, there is the view that public support for the war drops sharply with the first casualties and then declines more sedately, unless there are then sudden bursts of increased casualties, which cause correspondingly sharp falls in the level of public support for the war. This theory is termed "marginal casualties" and is associated with Scott Gartner and Gary Segura.[14]

In addition to these claims, there exists a set of explanations that the author terms "casualties plus politics." The first of these, associated with Eric Larsson, states that elite discord about the mission, along with casualties, are what cause public support to fall.[15] Elite discord most commonly means disagreement between the major parties but it could also mean public disagreement over the mission in the news media and upper reaches of the foreign service or military.

A different perspective claims that the public will tolerate casualties provided that the mission is based around restraining the aggressive foreign policy designs of a rival state—like the Gulf War of 1991—rather than around nation-building or counterinsurgency. This is known as the principal policy objective theory associated with Bruce Jentleson[16] and would suggest that the Afghan war lost popularity as it transformed from a straightforward defensive mission to extirpate al-Qaeda's bases post-9/11 to a more complex counterinsurgency and nation-building exercise.

Third, both academic analysts and news media pundits frequently suspect that a lack of multilateral backing for a mission may also be a key factor in causing support for it to fall. A lack of multilateral support for a mission may delegitimize it in the eyes of the peoples of participating nations,[17] it may also cause them to doubt the judgment of the leaders who took them into the war (because other leaders did not come to such a judgment),[18] or it may simply cause them to turn against the war out of resentment at the perceived "freeloading" of their allies.[19] Popular though it is to blame a lack of equitable, multilateral burden sharing for the decline in support for the Afghanistan war, it is problematic for several reasons. First, the Afghanistan war is authorized by a specific United Nations (UN) resolution,[20] and all leaders of the Western alliance at least publicly claim the war to be just and worthwhile. Second, it is very difficult to tell whether the perceived lack of multilateral burden sharing is really having an independent effect on the downward trajectory of support for the war or whether the unwillingness of some countries to contribute merely reflects the same factors that are causing public support for the war to drop in the main participating countries—such as the deteriorating progress of the war itself. Determining whether the lack of equitable burden sharing is actually having an effect in its own right requires a natural experiment—an instance in which a previous under contributor decided, for its own reasons, to ramp up its deployment. I argue that the reaction to the decision by France's President Nicholas Sarkozy to increase the French deployment to Afghanistan after his election in 2007 provides such a natural experiment, because this decision was essentially personal, not part of his election campaign, and did not reflect a sudden upsurge in France in support for the war or an improvement in the situation on the ground in Afghanistan.[21]

Finally, an increasingly popular view of the relationship between conflict and public opinion stresses that the public will be able to support military operations involving significant casualties only if they believe that the war will be won. This theory was developed by Peter Feaver, Christopher Gelpi, and Jason Reifler through close analysis of U.S. public opinion and the Iraq war[22] and is here first applied to the war in Afghanistan. Their work also suggests that the American public contains a segment of around 30 percent of "solid hawks" who will support a mission regardless of costs and who provide a "floor" below which public support will not fall.[23] This author argues that this explanation is the only one that works in all of the cases surveyed, even those such as Australia in which all other factors would suggest a different outcome to what we observe. This author also claims that the solid hawks, as identified, do have counterparts in other developed democracies and account for the interesting fact that in all of the countries surveyed (except Germany), once support hits the mid to low 30 percent level, it tends to flatten out and not decline further.

Consequently, the rising belief that the Afghanistan war will not and perhaps cannot be won, when combined with rising casualties, is the most important factor in causing public support to fall. If policymakers wish to halt or reverse this trend, turning around the public's perception of the likely outcome of the war is the key.

Additionally, this paper examines two other popular explanations for the decline in public support for the war that have developed in the news media, policy circles, and academia and were specifically inspired by the case of Afghanistan. The first of these "Afghanistan-specific" theories is that the unpopularity and perceived illegitimacy of the Iraq war has spread to the war in Afghanistan. As evidenced by the popular slogan "Bush lied, people died," this perspective suggests that the Iraq war destroyed the public's belief in the honesty and integrity of the existing political leadership and made them suspicious of any conflicts initiated by them, even if apparently unconnected to Iraq.[24] This author argues that if this theory holds water, one would expect to see the public's belief in the legitimacy of both conflicts decline at the same time and that if the leadership that initiated the Iraq war were to give way to a leadership that opposed Iraq but supported Afghanistan, we would see an increase in support for the latter conflict. In fact, evidence suggests that neither is the case and that the public is judging the Afghanistan war on its own merits, regardless of the situation in Iraq.

Also, it is widely held that the fall in support for the war derives from a poorly executed rhetorical strategy on the part of political leaders.[25] Leaders have often cycled through numerous rationales for the war—from counterterrorism to counternarcotics to humanitarianism and nation building to women's rights to helping one's allies and protecting the Western way of life. This has been accompanied by often vague and grandiose language. Critics charge that this has left Western publics confused and cynical about the true goals of the war. Far better, it is claimed, if leaders had simply stuck to a clear and simple rationale based on counterterrorism. This author contends that the evidence on this is mixed – most politicians have used the multiple rationales strategy at most times, so it is difficult to say what would have happened had they used some other strategy. Nonetheless, using many rationales probably has not helped politicians rally support for the war. Sticking to a clearer and more consistent rationale may *help* to stem the decline in support, but it will be insufficient by itself if the situation on the ground does not improve.

THE GOOD WAR? AMERICAN PUBLIC OPINION AND THE WAR IN AFGHANISTAN

The interaction between foreign policy and public opinion is better studied with respect to the United States than any other country on the planet. The vast majority of the academic casualty sensitivity literature is inspired by U.S. experiences and research with the American public. Moreover, American opinion on foreign policy is more extensively canvassed by pollsters than that of any other country.

One of the two major superpowers between 1945 and 1989, and the sole undisputed superpower of the post-Cold War world, the United States has engaged in numerous interventions since overcoming isolationist sentiment to enter World War II. U.S. forces have fought long wars in Korea, Vietnam, and Iraq, and launched numerous smaller interventions including Grenada, Panama, Lebanon, Somalia, Haiti, and Bosnia. The earliest studies of the impact of casualties on U.S. support for such interventions, such as John Mueller's, painted a picture of a highly casualty-sensitive public who were apt to abandon foreign policy missions very quickly once they became costly. This picture unquestionably influenced the beliefs not only of U.S. policymakers themselves, but also of American enemies such as Slobodan Milosevic, Saddam Hussein, and Osama bin Laden. Indeed, for all the U.S. news media commentary about European weakness that has emerged since 9/11, it is often forgotten that in the 1990s, it was the Americans who were believed to be the more casualty-sensitive. For example, when Belgian forces were withdrawn from Rwanda following a small number of deaths at the hands of the Hutu militias, UN Secretary-General Boutros Boutros Gali worried that the Belgians were becoming afflicted with "American syndrome: pull out at the first serious sign of trouble."[26]

Yet even before the Iraq and Afghanistan wars, this view of the American people as being unthinkingly casualty phobic had begun to be challenged by many authorities. Along with the theories developed by Larson and Jentleson which we have already discussed, empirical work also challenged the view that the entire U.S. public was beset by a crippling casualty "phobia." Steven Kull and Clay Ramsay disputed the conventional wisdom that U.S. withdrawal from Somalia resulted from the U.S. fatalities in the Black Hawk Down incident. Rather, they pointed out support had in fact been falling for some time beforehand.[27] In the Gulf War, moreover, they point out that public support for the mission never fell below 60 percent and in fact rose to 72 percent over the period in which the majority of the 148 American fatalities were sustained.[28] Likewise, a majority of the American public continued to support the U.S. troop presence in Saudi Arabia after 20 U.S. troops were killed at Dhahran airbase in a terrorist attack.[29] Hypothetical scenarios involving a substantial loss of life always saw sizeable majorities against subsequent withdrawal—with striking back and bringing in reinforcements being popular responses.[30] The realism of these responses had already been demonstrated after U.S. losses in Lebanon,[31] when a combination of replacing or increasing troops numbers, or taking punitive action against the perpetrators of attacks on U.S. troops, won out over the withdrawal option in public opinion polls. Opinion polls over the Kosovo campaign revealed a significant majority—60 percent—of the U.S. public were willing to incur 250 American casualties to push Serbian forces out of Kosovo.[32] Moreover, besides some blips at the beginning and the end of the Kosovo conflict, U.S. public support for the war mostly held up significantly above majority levels.[33] Although the conflict evinced lower support in the United States than in some European countries, it must be remembered that Kosovo was close to a purely "pro-bono" humanitarian intervention, without a clear link to a definite U.S. national interest, which many believed make the U.S. public more inclined to support military interventions.[34] Moreover, Kosovo was not in the United States' "backyard," as it was for the European countries.

Thus at the start of the Afghan war, U.S. public opinion could be predicted to be solid in the face of casualties, even if the conventional wisdom had for many years suggested otherwise. Another reason to suspect the United States to have a strong stomach for losses lies in the fact that it is the only country that was directly targeted by al-Qaeda on 9/11. Other countries, of course, sustained losses in the Twin Towers, and both Britain and Australia have subsequently suffered terrorist attacks of their own, but nothing has been on the same scale.

Public support for the Afghanistan war in the United States began at a stratospheric 89 percent, higher than in any of the other participating countries. The United States has paid by far the lion's share of the human cost of the Afghanistan war—1,080 Americans have lost their lives as part of Operation ENDURING FREEDOM, as of this writing.[35] Support has fallen by 40 percent over the course of the mission, and now most polls claim a majority favor withdrawal. The United States was the last country in which the war commanded majority support—but this is not because the fall in support has been less in the United States, but rather because support started from such a high base.

Casualties.

Let us first examine the claim that casualties alone are the key determinant.

Logarithmic Casualties. The extensive polls on the issue in the United States allow us to track the trajectory of American public opinion on Afghanistan with a great degree of accuracy. Unfortunately, as with all the other countries, the years between 2002 and 2005 are largely a "black hole" as Afghanistan dropped off the political radar to be replaced by the much more controversial war in Iraq. Nonetheless, a graph of U.S. polling results on Afghanistan over time is still instructive (see Figures 1 and 2).

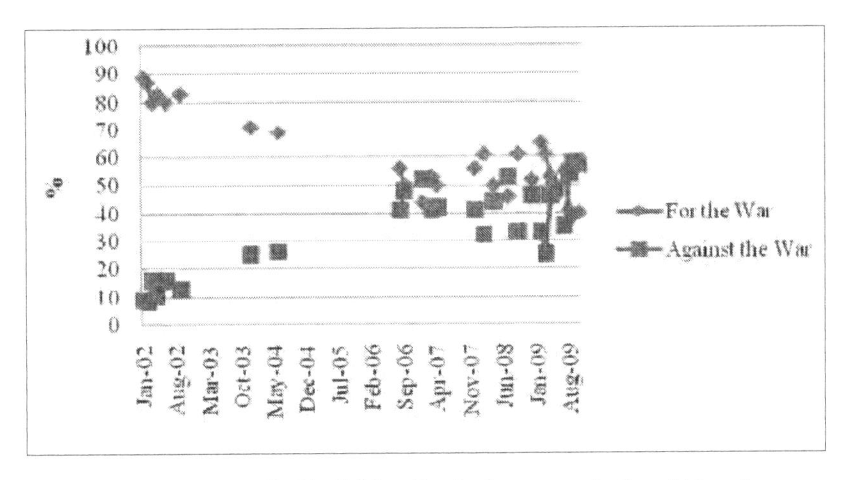

Figure 1: U.S. Public Opinion and the War in Afghanistan, 2002-09.

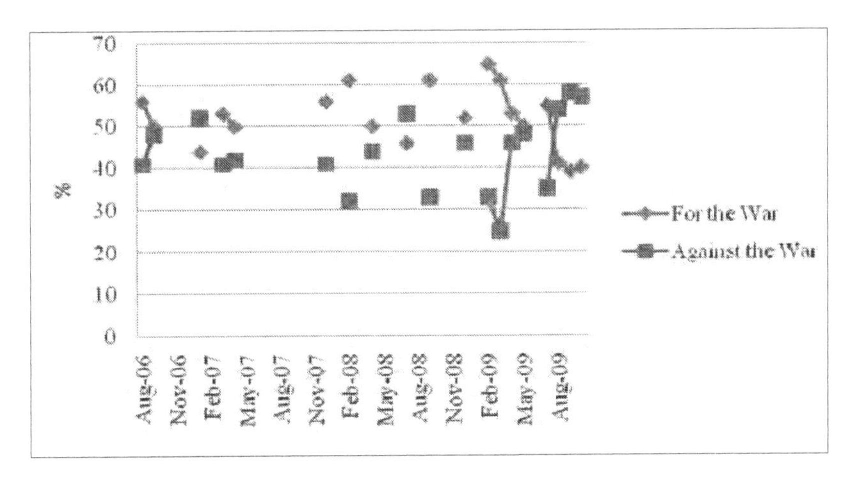

Figure 2. U.S. Public Opinion and the War in Afghanistan, 2006-09.

As can be seen from examining the two figures above, the U.S. data do not fit the logarithmic theory well. Instead of a sharp drop followed by a gradual decline, there appears to be a relatively steady linear decline before the revival of the Taliban insurgency in 2005-06, followed by a reasonably turbulent period since then, with the majority of public opinion almost certainly now opposed with some more room to fall.

If public support is not a straightforward logarithmic function of casualties, does the other pure casualty sensitivity explanation work any better?

Marginal Casualties. The relative abundance of polling data and the high number of U.S. casualties allow us to plot the respective courses of U.S. casualties and public opinion. Figure 3 gives an overview from 2001-2009, while Figures 4 and 5 break the figures down between 2006-07 and 2008-09 to give a closer and more detailed picture.

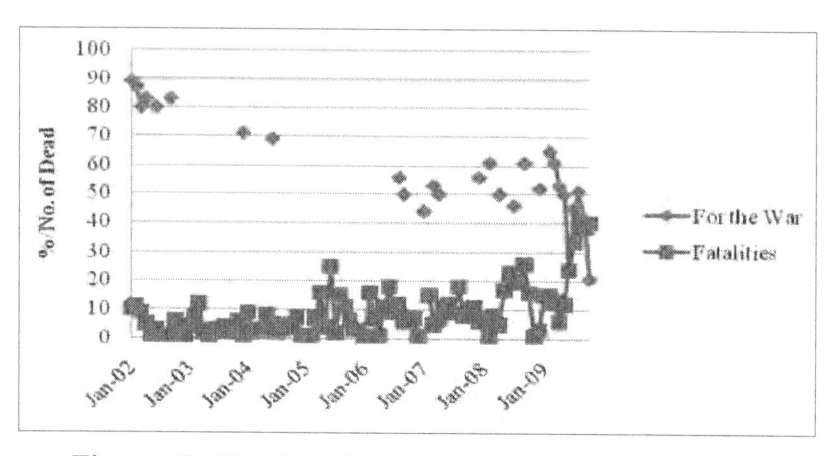

Figure 3. U.S. Public Support for the War and Fatalities, 2001-09.

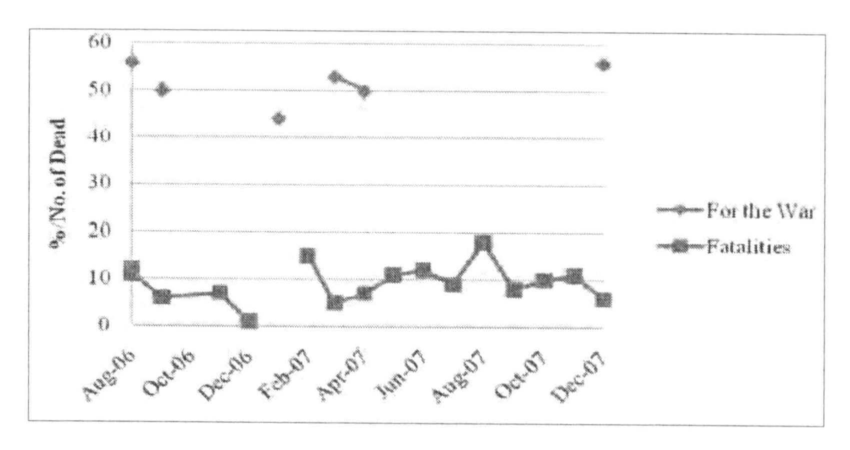

Figure 4. U.S. Public Support for the War and Fatalities, 2006-07.

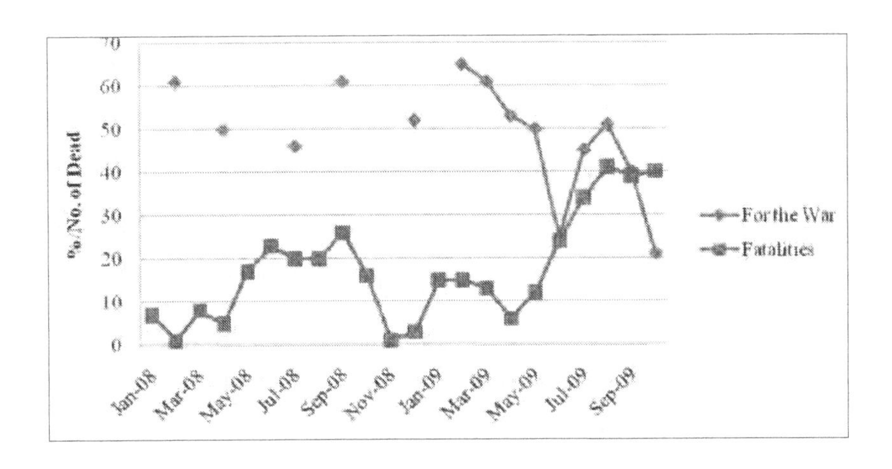

Figure 5. U.S. Public Support for the War and Fatalities, 2008-09.

As can be seen most clearly from Figures 3, 4, and 5, casualties alone cannot account for the trajectory of U.S. support for Afghanistan. Especially in 2008 and 2009, U.S. public support for the war has seen relatively steep mini-declines at times of stable or declining casualties. The spike in casualties over the summer of 2008 did produce a slight drop in support, but this drop is much shallower than the drop in early 2009, when casualties were declining. Moreover, a second spike in late summer 2008 appears to have produced an *increase* in U.S. public support for the war. Looking further back, late 2006 and early 2007 saw a relatively substantial decline in support at a time of stable and decreasing casualties. Finally, while casualties held steady over the summer of 2009, support plummeted. In other words, a detailed look at the timeline of U.S. support for the war provides little support for the idea that casualties alone have caused support to fall. Clearly some other factors besides casualties must be at play.

Casualties Plus Politics.

Elite Consensus. From the beginning, the Afghan war enjoyed bipartisan support in the United States as it had in Britain and Australia.[36] Indeed, as partisan divisions increased over Iraq, many Democrats rushed to declare their support for the Afghanistan war as a truly just, legal, and defensive "war of necessity" in contrast to Iraq. Although Senator John Kerry's own voting record on the Iraq war stopped him from drawing the same kind of contrast later drawn by other Democrats, he did condemn Bush's perceived neglect of Afghanistan during his run for President in 2004:

> Nowhere is the need for collective endeavor greater than in Afghanistan. We must end the Bush administration's delay in expanding NATO forces and deploying them outside of Kabul. We must accelerate the training for the Afghan army and police. The disarmament of the warlord militias and their reintegration into society must be transformed from a pilot program into a mainstream strategy. Either the warlords must be drawn into a closer relationship with the central government, or they need to be isolated.[37]

This theme was picked up even more strongly by the next Democratic presidential candidate, Barack Obama, in 2008. During a live televised debate with Republican John McCain in Oxford Mississippi, Obama famously stated that:

> We took our eye off the ball. . . . We took our eye off Afghanistan. We took our eye off the folks who perpetrated 9/11. They are still sending out videotapes.[38]

Indeed, at times over the course of the Bush presidency, it often appeared that Democratic leaders were more in favor of the Afghanistan war than the ruling Republicans. The vast majority of Republicans, in turn, were unquestionably foursquare in favor of the war, at least when Bush was still in the White House.[39] Until the spring of 2009, congressional opposition mostly consisted only of left-wing mavericks such as Dennis Kucinich[40] and libertarian isolationists such as Ron Paul.[41] Thus the United States enjoyed a high degree of elite consensus, arguably higher than in any of the other countries under study. The misgivings about the war voiced increasingly openly by congressional Democrats from the spring of 2009 onwards[42] followed rather than preceded the largest drops in support, and were arguably more a consequence than a cause of it. The same is also true of the very public hesitation of President Barack Obama to act on the leaked recommendations of the McChrystal Report—a fact from which the public could easily infer (rightly or wrongly) both waning presidential enthusiasm for the war and potentially deep divisions between the Obama administration and its military advisers.[43] Public support has fallen since the leak, but it was already on a stark downward spiral beforehand.

At the same time, the United States has not seen anything similar to the extra-political anti-war movement that has emerged in Britain. Popular foreign policy experts such as Fareed Zakaria,[44] Peter Bergen,[45] and Thomas Friedman (until late 2009)[46] struck a very similar note to Australian experts such as David Kilcullen—acknowledging the gravity of the situation but maintaining the belief that victory is still within the Allies' grasp. Bergen, for example, stated that:

> The United States can neither precipitously withdraw from Afghanistan nor help foster the emergence of a

> stable Afghan state by doing it on the cheap; the consequence would be the return of the Taliban and al-Qaeda. Fortunately, the U.S. is not alone; unlike in Iraq, there is an international coalition of forty-two countries in Afghanistan supporting NATO efforts there, with troops or other assistance. Even Muslim countries are part of this mix. Turkey, for instance, ran the International Security Assistance Force in Afghanistan in 2005, and the United Arab Emirates and Jordan have both sent small numbers of soldiers. The United States overthrew the Taliban in the winter of 2001. It has a moral obligation to ensure that when it does leave Afghanistan it does so secure in the knowledge that the country will never again be a launching pad for the world's deadliest terrorist groups, and that the country is on the way to a measure of stability and prosperity. When that happens, it is not too fanciful to think that Afghanistan's majestic mountains, verdant valleys, and jasmine-scented gardens may once again draw the tourists that once flocked there.[47]

Even a number of avowedly left-wing American commentators have been reluctant to advocate withdrawal from Afghanistan. The *Atlantic Monthly*'s Matthew Yglesias, author of "Heads in the Sand: How the Republicans screw up American Foreign Policy and Foreign Policy Screws up the Democrats," as late as July 2009 wrote about "A Winnable War in Afghanistan."[48]

The conversion of conservative columnist George Will, as well as Friedman, from support for to opposition to the war attracted a good deal of news media attention precisely because they were two of the first major mainstream news media figures to oppose the war—however Friedman's and Will's about-face, like the discontent among congressional Democrats, came well into the precipitous decline in support that has characterized 2009.[49]

On these grounds, the United States should unquestionably be considered as a country enjoying elite consensus over Afghanistan, at least until after public support had already entered a steep decline. Elite discord over the war in Afghanistan is a symptom, not a cause, of the war's declining popularity.

Multilateralism. According to the "natural experiment," identified earlier to gauge the effect of multilateral burden-sharing on the trajectory of support for the war, we should expect to see U.S. support for the war rise, at least temporarily, after the decision by President Sarkozy to increase the French military presence in Afghanistan in March 2007. However, a look at U.S. polling data suggests that the French deployment went largely unnoticed—U.S. support for the war fell by 3 percent between March and April 2007.[50] There is very little evidence to suggest that a lack of support for the war from America's allies has exerted a significant downward effect on U.S. public support for the war independently of all the other factors at play.

Principal Policy Objective. The United States is the one case in which we can extensively evaluate the importance of the changing principal policy objective on support for the war. Whereas polling data for all other countries stops in early 2002 shortly after the success of the initial invasion, U.S. polls continue into the period between the initial invasion and the Taliban revival in 2005. This period is instructive, as the Afghanistan war was still perceptibly going well, and casualties were low, but the nature of the mission was closer to one of internal political change. The changing principal policy objective does have some effect then—for support fell between 10 and 14 percent between 2002 and 2004. This suggests that moving from a straightforwardly defensive restraint mission to a nation-building exercise may have exerted some downward pressure on the trajectory of support in the United States at least. Of course, a significant fall in support between 2002 and 2004 is also consistent with contagion from the Iraq war, but there is, in fact, little evidence in favor of this alternative explanation, as we shall see for various reasons cited below.

Prospects for Success. The prospects for success of the mission on the ground are clearly a key part of the explanation for the trajectory of public support for the war in the United States. The drops in support for the war over the last 8 years, which are inexplicable purely in terms of casualties, track very well to incoming information about the fortunes of the American and Allied war effort.

Starting in 2006, the resurgence of the Taliban not only surprised public opinion and the news media in the United States, but caused them to rapidly revise their estimate of the prospects of success for the war—from already won to potentially loseable. Thus *The Washington Post*'s May 2006 editorial stated:

> The heavy fighting in Afghanistan during the past week, in which more than 300 people have died, may seem like a sudden eruption to many Americans—*who tend to assume the war there ended, more or less, years ago*. . . . The U.S.-led effort to transform this onetime base of al-Qaeda is far from over; in fact, it is still just beginning.[51]

The next poll after this editorial revealed support for the war had dropped to 56 percent,[52], 13 percent lower than when the question had last been asked in 2004[53]—and one of the largest reductions in the entire 8 years.

Moving a little forward in time, the winter of 2006 saw a raft of negative stories and assessments of the

Afghan situation in the U.S. news media. In December 2006, the *Los Angeles Times* editorialized that "all the indicators for Afghanistan are headed south." *Newsweek* reported that "much of Afghanistan appears to be failing again," and Senator John Kerry warned that "we are losing Afghanistan."[54] In January 2010, James L. Jones, President Obama's future National Security Advisor, authored a report stating: "Make no mistake, NATO is not winning in Afghanistan."[55] Significantly, the first poll taken after these assessments and CIA director Michael Hayden's gloomy testimony to Congress about the progress of the war in November 2006 was the first to show majority opposition to the war in the United States.[56] In fact, September 2006 to January 2007 saw a 16 percent drop in support—one of the sharpest falls of the entire period.

The sharpest drops, however, have occurred since the spring of 2009. Shortly after the election of President Obama, support experienced a temporary boost (more of this later), but this boost has more than disappeared since February, with a greater than 15 percent drop in support since then. In 2009, a fresh round of pessimistic assessments of the situation on the ground, as well as a demonstration by the Taliban of their ability to keep on fighting through the winter, appeared, while in previous years fighting had abated between the fall and spring. In mid-February, Obama's appointee to Afghanistan, veteran diplomat Richard Holbrooke sounded the following warning:

> First of all, the victory, as defined in purely military terms, is not achievable and I cannot stress that too highly.[57]

Obama's inaugural address, in which he spoke of "achieving a hard fought peace"[58] rather than a "victory," struck a similar note.

The summer and early fall of 2009 have also witnessed a number of events that have caused the U.S. public to revise their estimation of the prospects for success in Afghanistan even further downwards—the widely reported fraud and violence accompanying the summer re-election of Hamid Karzai,[59] and, of course, most obviously the McChrystal Report, which stated that "failure to gain the initiative and reverse insurgent momentum in the near term (next 12 months) . . . risks an outcome where defeating the insurgency is no longer possible.[60]" As one would expect if prospects for success were a key factor, support for the war, which was already falling sharply in the spring, has nosedived in the summer and early fall.

Undoubtedly, then, one simply cannot understand the drop in support for the war in the United States without considering the impact of the rapidly deteriorating situation on the ground in Afghanistan since 2005 alongside mounting U.S. casualties. This does not, however, exclude the possibility that other factors could also be at play. We will now proceed to examine the importance of the Iraq war and the changing rhetoric of American leaders on public support for the war.

Afghanistan-Specific Explanations.

Iraq War Contagion. It is in the case of the United States that we can see most clearly how the "contagion" effect from the Iraq war might play itself out. Not only do we have a change of government from a pro- to an anti-Iraq war administration, but extensive polling data allows us to track public attitudes of both wars over time.

In favor of the contention that Iraq lowered support for the war in Afghanistan is the spike in support for the Afghan war when the anti-Iraq war President Barack Obama replaced the pro-Iraq war President George W Bush. The first poll on the war since Obama's election put support for the war at 65 percent,[61] a full 13 percent higher than in the last poll in December.[62] However, this spike in support swiftly dissipated, as we have seen above. Moreover, the last poll prior to December had put support much higher, at 61 percent, not far from the February figure.[63] As a glance at the timeline shows, polling figures were very volatile over 2008, and it is not clear that the apparent blip over Obama's election is more than a brief rally effect associated with the election of a new President. Only since the beginning of 2009 have polling figures shown a consistent trend—downwards.

Moreover, polling data about the U.S. public's attitude to the Iraq and Afghanistan wars suggests that they have been able to separate them very effectively, as Figures 6 and 7 demonstrate.

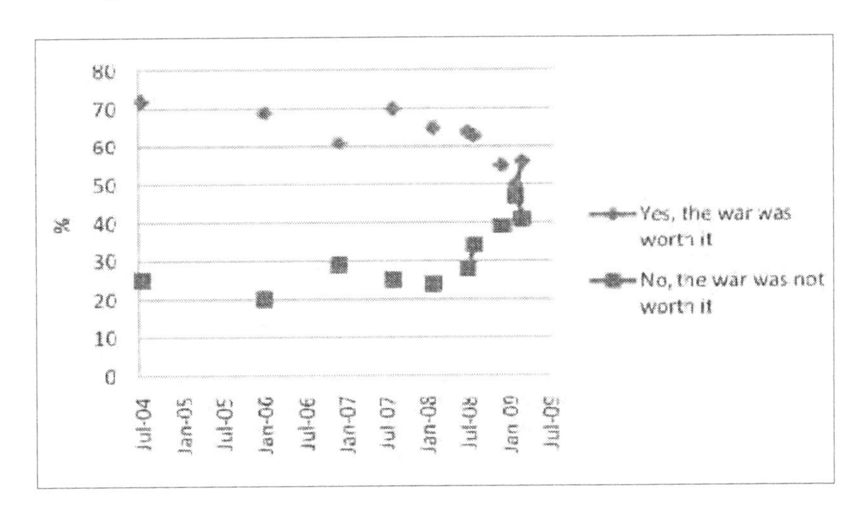

Figure 6. U.S. Retrospective Opinion on the War in Afghanistan, 2004-09.

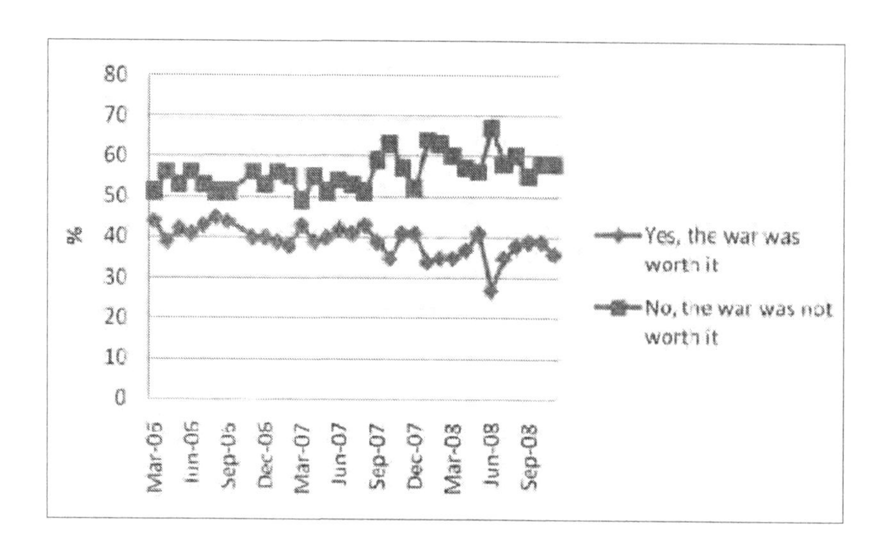

Figure 7. U.S. Retrospective Opinion on the War in Iraq, 2006-09.

As can be seen from Figure 6, the belief in the justification of the Afghanistan war has held up remarkably well over the last few years. Polls from March 2009 still put this belief at 56 percent,[64] little different from the level at December 2006,[65] though down somewhat from when the question was first asked in June 2004 (then at 72 percent).[66] By contrast, the belief that the war in Iraq was justified dropped well below majority levels years beforehand, as can be seen from Figure 7. The belief that the Iraq war was the right thing to do has not held the support of even a plurality of Americans since the summer of 2005. The key change with regard to the Iraq war came about over 2004-05, yet in that same year belief in the justification of the war in Afghanistan seems barely to have moved.[67]

Thus it appears that, contrary to much news media and political opinion, the Iraq war has had little damaging effect on the war in Afghanistan—rather it seems that the American public has judged each war on its respective merits. The only evidence to the contrary is the apparent increase in support for the war at the time of Barack Obama's inauguration, but it is not clear that this increase was genuinely significant or more than a mere blip. Even assuming it was not random noise, there are other potential explanations for the mini "Obama surge." We will examine this now.

Confused Rationale. The Bush administration charted a middle course in terms of its rhetorical strategy on Afghanistan. First, as public support in the United States was initially higher than in other countries and the war enjoyed strong support from the Democrats, the administration devoted far more time to justifying the much more controversial Iraq war. When Bush did talk about Afghanistan, however, he mostly maintained the counterterrorism line.[68] In 2006, for example, Bush stated:

> And from the beginning, our actions in Afghanistan have had a clear purpose-in other words, our goals are clear for people to understand-and that is to rid that country of the Taliban and the terrorists, and build a lasting free society that will be an ally in the war on terror.[69]

In a speech to the American Enterprise Institute in 2007, Bush delivered essentially the same message:

> Our goal in Afghanistan is to help the people of that country to defeat the terrorists and establish a stable, moderate, democratic state that respects the rights of its citizens, governs its territory effectively, and is a reliable ally in this war against extremists and terrorists.[70]

Again in August 2008 to a Gathering of Veterans of Foreign Wars, Bush gave a very similar rationale for the war, mentioning the development of Afghanistan's democracy and economy but only because these are seen to be crucial to preventing the resurgence of the Taliban and the reestablishment of a base for al-Qaeda:

> In Afghanistan, we removed a dangerous regime that harbored the terrorists who plotted the attacks of 9/11. Because we acted, the Afghan people have been liberated, and a nation that was once a training ground for terrorists has become an ally in the war on terror. . . . We will ensure Afghanistan never again becomes a safe haven for those seeking to launch attacks on America and our allies.[71]

Yet at times during his Presidency Bush departed from the stark simplicity of a counterterrorism message and resorted to talking points about democratization, development, and human rights similar to those of the British and Canadians. In March 2008, meeting a returning commander from Afghanistan in the White House, Bush stated:

> As you can see here on the screen in front of me, we've got assembled in Afghanistan-thanks to Ambassador Wood-PRTs, which is Provincial Reconstruction Teams, made up of military and civilian personnel, all aiming to help the Afghans recover from unbelievable brutality of the Taliban and have a society that's capable of meeting the needs of its people. We've also got two members of the PRT here present with us. Our strategy in Afghanistan is, one, to provide enough security so civil society can move forward. Any counter-effective counter-insurgency strategy will require more than just military action; it requires a military-civilian interface. And so if you look on the screen, you see brave and courageous Americans in uniform and not in uniform, because they're a part of this strategy to help Afghans, one, understand the blessings of good governance. In other words, the folks are attempting to fight corruption at the local level so that the local citizens are able to have a positive outlook

> about their government. We're also working to educate people, build roads, provide good health care. And our fellow citizens are there on the ground, in some difficult circumstances, all aiming to help this young democracy survive and thrive. And there are difficulties, but we're also making progress. And the best thing we got going for us-not only do we have brave and compassionate citizens willing to serve, but we've also got an ideology based upon liberty, which stands in stark contrast to the ideology of the thugs and murderers called the Taliban. And the job at hand is to help these folks recover, help the Afghans realize there's a better future for them. And it's hard work, but it's necessary work for the security of our country.[72]

In another example, during his weekly radio address in October 2006, Bush touched on humanitarianism and nation-building alongside counterterrorism in his description of the Afghan conflict:

> In Afghanistan, President Karzai continues the work of building a safer and brighter future for his nation. Today, forces from more than 40 countries, including members of the NATO Alliance, are bravely serving side by side with Afghan forces. These forces are fighting the extremists who want to bring down the free Government that the people of Afghanistan have established. America and its allies will continue to stand with the people of Afghanistan as they defend their democratic gains. Working with President Karzai's Government, we will defeat the enemies of a free Afghanistan and help the Afghan people build a nation that will never again oppress them or be a safe haven for terrorists.[73]

In a speech to the Reserve Officer's Association, Bush again stressed building Afghan democracy alongside counterterrorism in his outline of the reasons for U.S. involvment:

> So after liberating Afghanistan, we began the difficult work of helping the Afghan people rebuild their country, and establish a free nation on the rubble of the Taliban's tyranny. With the help of the United Nations and coalition countries, the Afghan leaders chose a interim government, they wrote and approved a democratic constitution, they held elections to choose a new president and they elected leaders to represent them in a new parliament. In those parliamentary elections, more than 6 million Afghans defied terrorist threats and cast their ballots. They made it clear they wanted to live in a free society. As I travel around the country, I tell people that I'm not surprised when people say, "I want to live in liberty." I believe liberty is universal. I believe deep within the soul of every man, woman and child on the face of the Earth is the desire to live in freedom. And when we free people, we not only do our duty to ourselves, but we help the rise of decent human beings. As Afghans have braved the terrorists and claimed their freedom, we've helped them. And we will continue to help them. It's in our interests that we help this young democracy survive and grow strong. We helped them build security forces they need to defend their democratic gains. In the past five years, our coalition has trained and equipped more than 30,000 soldiers in the Afghan national army. And at this moment, several thousand more are in training at a Kabul military training center. [74]

It is fair to say, then, that Bush's rhetoric on Afghanistan, while always mentioning the Afghan conflict as part of the broader struggle against terrorism, has not always consistently stuck to a narrow counterterrorism rationale for the Afghan mission.

Indeed, President Obama's rhetoric since assuming power has clearly been influenced by the confused rationale explanation for the falling support for the Afghan war. Obama and other members of his administration have self-consciously sought to distance themselves from the multiple rationales that characterized earlier justifications for the war both in the United States and overseas.

The following exchange between PBS's Jim Lehrer and Obama in February 2008 illustrates this well:

> JIM LEHRER: And you also said in your speech that it's - one of the lessons of Iraq is that there are clearly defined goals. What are the goals for Afghanistan right now?
>
> BARACK OBAMA: Well, I don't think that they're clear enough, that's part of the problem. We've seen a sense of drift in the mission in Afghanistan, and that's why I've ordered a head-to-toe, soup-to-nuts review of our approach in Afghanistan.
>
> Now, I can articulate some very clear, minimal goals in Afghanistan, and that is that we make sure that it's not a safe haven for al Qaeda, they are not able to launch attacks of the sort that happened on 9/11 against the American homeland or American interests. How we achieve that initial goal, what kinds of strategies and tactics we need to put in place, I don't think that we've thought it through, and we haven't used the entire arsenal of American power.[75]

Likewise in March 2009, in his statement on the new strategy for Afghanistan and Pakistan, Obama stated:

> Many people in the United States—and many in partner countries that have sacrificed so much—have a simple question: What is our purpose in Afghanistan? After so many years, they ask, why do our men and women still fight and die there? And they deserve a straightforward answer. So let me be clear: al Qaeda and its allies—the terrorists who planned and supported the 9/11 attacks—are in Pakistan and Afghanistan. Multiple intelligence estimates have warned that al Qaeda is actively planning attacks on the United States homeland from its safe haven in Pakistan. And if the Afghan government falls to

> the Taliban—or allows al Qaeda to go unchallenged—that country will again be a base for terrorists who want to kill as many of our people as they possibly can.[76]

Speaking on CNN's AC360 program in July 2009, Obama reiterated the overriding importance of counterterrorism as the goal of the Afghanistan operation:

> I want to make sure that we have got the best possible strategy to succeed in a very limited aim, and that is to ensure that al Qaeda and its allies cannot launch attacks on the U.S. homeland and on U.S. interests.[77]

Secretary of Defense Bob Gates in February 2009 echoed Obama's deliberate framing of the strategic goal in pure counterterrorism terms:

> Our primary goal is to prevent Afghanistan from being used as a base for terrorists and extremists to attack the United States and its allies.[78]

If the lack of one clear and consistent rationale for the war is a key factor driving the fall in support for the war in the United States, then one would surely expect to see something of a revival in support since the election of President Obama. In office is an administration that explicitly buys into the clear rationale theory and shapes its own rhetoric accordingly—stressing only counterterrorism and minimalist goals. So far, however, the results have been disappointing. As we have seen, support for the war has hemorrhaged consistently since Obama's inauguration. This does not necessarily mean that the confused rationale theory is not valid, because many other things such as casualties and the deteriorating situation on the ground in Afghanistan have been trending towards a drop in public support.

Moreover, as Janice Stein has pointed out, Obama has sometimes strayed from the more disciplined rhetorical strategy he set out for himself— for example, by commenting on Afghan domestic policies regarding women's rights.[79] At the same time, however, a distinction can be fairly drawn between the unprompted and frequent deployment of numerous rationales by political leaders such as Canada's Bill Graham and Britain's John Reid (see the Canadian and British sections), and Obama's occasional deviations from a strictly security-based rationale. For example, Obama's well-known description of Afghan legislation allegedly legalizing marital rape within minority Shi'a communities as "abhorent" was a response to a journalist rather than a deliberately scripted set piece speech. Moreover, Obama made clear in the same answer that the aim of Afghan operation was still U.S. national security and that the new legislation would not affect this goal.[80]

Conversely, critics such as Peter Feaver have claimed that Obama's lack of public statements on Afghanistan in the late spring and summer of 2009 have also served to undermine public support.[81] It is true that the sharp drop in public support for the war coincided with Obama's silence on the subject prior to the West Point address. Moreover, public support for the war did increase marginally in December 2009, once Obama had returned to addressing the issue of Afghanistan. However, it is not clear that this increase was anything more than another random blip—there had been a far larger apparent increase in support for the war in the previous month of November, before the West Point address.[82] Indeed, if Obama's apparent lack of focus on the war in the middle of 2009 did affect support for the war, it was only to undo the short rally which had accompanied his assumption of power and return public support for the war to the same levels it had been in the final months of the Bush administration.

In the U.S. case at least, however, the evidence suggests that a clear and consistent rationale for the war may be a necessary, but not sufficient, condition for the fall in public support to be arrested. The Obama administration clearly believes that one consistent, security-based rationale is key to reviving support, and has shaped its rhetoric accordingly. So far, however, without a clear turnaround in the situation on the ground to accompany the rhetorical shift, the results have been disappointing. Indeed, sharper rhetoric justifying the war solely in terms of counterterrorism has simply drawn renewed attention to the attractiveness of alternative strategies, which promise to achieve the end of counterterrorism at (so their proponents claim) lower cost—such as the "light footprint" approach based on special forces and predator drones favored by Vice-President Biden,[83] or a complete withdrawal from Afghanistan and a reliance instead on tighter border control and internal security to combat al Qaeda, as the United States and others "circle the wagons."

Conclusion. A variety of factors explain the drop in support for the Afghanistan war in the United States. Yet at the same time, some explanations that one might have suspected to be useful have little empirical support. Clearly, casualties do not tell the whole story. At the same time, elite discord is a consequence rather than a cause of the fall in support for the war, while there is no evidence that the perceived lack of support from America's allies has had a significant independent effect.

The deteriorating course of the war on the ground and the shift in the nature of the mission from a straightforward restraint mission in the aftermath of 9/11 to a murkier counterinsurgency, however, are unquestionably key factors. A fall in public approval of the Afghan war accompanies the change in the nature of the engagement in 2002 from a purely defensive war against al Qaeda to a nation-building exercise. The same is also true of pessimistic and gloomy assessments of the situation on the ground—grim prognostications from generals, envoys, and agents hit public support harder even than sharp casualty spikes.

At the same time, Iraq has had little impact on public perceptions of Afghanistan, a finding that is surprising. Polling data over time shows the American people quite able and willing to compartmentalize the two wars. Similarly, the claim that the confused and shifting rationale for the war is the key factor can be doubted. A clearer strategic rationale accompanied by a deteriorating situation on the ground has done little to stem the hemorrhage of support; instead it has simply prompted many to ask the question as to whether the clear and limited goal of counterterrorism could not be achieved in a more cost-effective manner than through a fully-fledged counterinsurgency.

THE "DEPUTY SHERIFF"—AUSTRALIAN PUBLIC OPINION AND THE AFGHAN WAR

An examination of Australian history and the attitudes of the Australian people towards the United States and towards the use of force prior to 9/11 would lead one to predict that Australia would be a rock steady U.S. ally in the forthcoming conflict.

The Australian public has been accustomed to Australian forces fighting in distant interventions even before Australia's independence from Britain (termed Federation in Australia) in 1901.[84] Forces from the Australian states participated in British imperial interventions in the Sudan, New Zealand, the Boer War, and World Wars I and II.[85] Indeed, one of the foundational events of Australian national identity happened not in Australia itself, but in a military operation in the Middle East on behalf of the British Empire—Gallipoli. The Australian and New Zealand Army Corps (ANZAC) Day, commemorating the Gallipoli landings, is arguably Australia's most important national day.[86] Although the legacy of the Gallipoli operation habituates Australians to the idea of their military fighting in distant interventions with their allies, it also has implanted a national myth of Australian lives being sacrificed for the benefit of others in conflicts not relevant to the Australian national interest.[87]

Following World War II, Australia has been the most consistent U.S. ally. Australian troops have fought alongside Americans in Korea[88] and Vietnam,[89] as well as the Gulf War of 1991[90] and Operation IRAQI FREEDOM in 2003.[91] Australia has also spearheaded international interventions to restore order in neighboring islands such as East Timor[92] and the Solomons.[93]

The upshot of Australia's long and proud military tradition is, however, mostly a robust public attitude to the use of force overseas. Although Australia did not participate in Kosovo or Bosnia, and the Pew Global Poll on the legitimacy of military force did not include Australia, some indication of preexisting Australian attitudes can be gleamed by looking at opinion on the East Timor intervention. In spite of explicit warnings of Australian fatalities from Prime Minister John Howard in advance of the operation, fully 72 percent of Australians supported the dispatch of Australian troops to the island.[94]

Australia is often described as one of the most pro-American countries in the world.[95] Fellow English-speaking democracies, comrades in arms in numerous conflicts with a classless frontier society ethic setting them apart from Great Britain, Australia and the United States are thought to have much in common. This impressionistic judgment is backed up by hard data. Although Pew Global did not canvass Australian opinion on the United States, the Australian state broadcaster ABC did participate in the "What the World thinks of America" Project. Australia exhibited a net favorability rating of the United States of 64 percent, 10 percent above the average and higher than any other country in the survey except for Canada, the UK, and Israel. A net 58 percent of Australians agreed that the United States was a force for good in the world, 13 percent higher than the sample average and higher than every other country apart from Canada and Israel. Moreover, 56 percent of Australians agreed that the United States is a beacon of hope and opportunity, again 6 percent higher than average and lower only than Canada, the UK, and Israel. Conversely, 56 percent of Australians also agreed that the United States is reaping the thorns sown by its rulers, but this is 4 percent below average and lower than any other country other than the UK and Israel.[96]

Thus, John Howard must have felt a high degree of confidence in the strength of Australian public support for the Afghan war when he first deployed Australian forces there in 2001.[97] Since 2001, the fatalities for Australia have been very low in comparison with the other participating countries; 11 Australian soldiers have lost their lives in Afghanistan.[98] The low level of Australian casualties does not reflect a reluctance to serve in the danger zone of southern Afghanistan. Surprisingly, given its history and closeness to the United States, the Australian Defense Force does operate under some parliamentary caveats; however, these caveats are far less restrictive than those of Germany. It is understood that the Australian caveats require that Australian forces not be deployed outside of Uruzgan province without specific approval from Canberra.[99] However, Uruzgan is a predominantly Pashtun area and, although quieter than many other southern provinces, is still part of the heartland of the Taliban insurgency.[100] Thus Australia's low casualties are a function of the smaller size of the Australian deployment, which for most of the history of the conflict consisted mostly of Special Air Service (SAS) special forces.[101] Some polls have indicated that Australian support for the war has held up well—as late as June 2008, Pew Global polls were showing support levels as high as 61 percent for the operation.[102] Even this year, polls for Australian National University showed a very small majority in favor of the operation.[103] Most polls, however, now show majority opposition and have done so since 2008. The month after Pew's poll, the respected Sydney-based think tank, the Lowy Institute, conducted a poll that revealed 57 percent opposition to the war.[104] The same think tank's annual report the previous year had yielded an even 46-46 percent split between supporters and opponents.[105] In April 2009, a further commercial poll stated that only 38 percent of Australians supported keeping troops in Afghanistan, close to British levels of support.[106] A March 2009 poll for *The Australian* newspaper did not ask whether respondents wished to maintain existing troops on the ground, but did reveal that 65 percent of Australians are opposed to sending any reinforcements.[107] Although Australian polls have thus been frustratingly contradictory, it is a reasonable bet to say that support, having once been very high, is now much lower, probably less than 50 percent.

How much do casualties alone account for the fall in support in the Australian case?

Casualties.

Unfortunately, the scarce and scattered Australian polls do not allow us to track the response of public opinion to casualties as we did in the American case. The Australian polling gap is much longer and larger than its equivalents in the other English-speaking countries. The contradictory nature of the polls cited above means that it is difficult even to trace when the sharpest drops in support occurred. However, the fact that there now exists Australian polls that indicate majority opposition to the war is problematic for any pure casualty sensitivity theory. Other countries taking similar numbers of casualties earlier in the war did not see significant drops in public support.

The first such Australian polls showing majority opposition occurred at a point when Australia had suffered only five casualties. By the time Canada had passed the same threshold as a percentage of their total military forces, Canadian support was at the same level it had been in the immediate aftermath of 9/11.[108]

One can only interpret this fact in two ways. Either Australia has a lower preexisting casualty tolerance than Canada, which is unlikely, or Australian casualties had a heavier effect on public opinion because they came at a later stage of the operation, when the prospects for the war had worsened. In either event, casualties alone cannot account for the difference.

Casualties Plus Politics.

Elite Consensus. Like the British and American cases, the Afghan war has enjoyed bipartisan support ever since 2001. The Labor opposition supported John Howard's initial decision to go to war in 2001,[109] and when Labor's Kevin Rudd replaced Howard in December 2007, he pledged to continue Australia's deployment in Afghanistan even while withdrawing Australian troops from Iraq.[110] Political opposition to the Afghan war, as in the United States and Great Britain, has been confined to minority left-wing parties such as the Australian Greens.[111]

Moreover, unlike Great Britain, Australia does not have a strong extra-parliamentary opposition to the war among foreign affairs, security, and area specialists. The only "greybeard" to have registered his misgivings is former Liberal Prime Minister Malcolm Fraser:

> I would desperately like to think that President Obama's approach can work but I suspect it won't work unless people can talk with those elements of the Taliban who are not al-Qaida and they are not all, as I am advised.[112]

However, the Australian news media debate has more been characterized by a large number of expert voices in favor of the war. David Kilcullen, who as an academic, former military officer, and adviser to General David Petraeus in Iraq, is, in many ways, the closest Australian counterpart to Rory Stewart, has garnered large amounts of news media attention with a grim but ultimately still positive message on Afghanistan. Kilcullen, in contrast to Stewart, believes that the war is still just about winnable and has set out in a long series of articles and books how he believes it can be won:

> The situation in Afghanistan is dire. But the war is winnable. We need to focus our attention on the problem, and think before acting. But we need to think fast, and our actions need to involve a major change of direction, focusing on securing the population rather than chasing the enemy, and delivering effective legitimate governance to the people, bottom-up, at the local level. Do that, do it fast, and we stand an excellent chance of turning things around.[113]

In a similar vein, the well respected former Labor Foreign Minister Gareth Evans, now full time at the International Crisis Group think tank, has emphasized that the Afghan situation is grave, but underlined that a withdrawal would be catastrophic:

> As a reinvigorated insurgency threatens the gains that have been made, and Western capitals, pressured by publics unwilling to accept military casualties, begin to explore endgames and exit strategies, the risk of losing Afghanistan is very real. . . . If the international community does not stay the course in Afghanistan the price could be inordinately high.[114]

Former Defense Secretary in the same Labor administration, Kim Beazley, has also gone on the record stressing his support for the Australian mission. A highly regarded voice in security and foreign affairs and current Professor of International Relations at the University of Western Australia, Beazley offered public words of advice to Prime Minister Rudd:

> With the additional commitment the Prime Minister announced the appointment of Ric Smith, retired diplomat and Defence Department Secretary, to the position of Special Envoy to Afghanistan and Pakistan. This move will elevate in the public mind the broader aspects of our Afghanistan commitment. Afghanistan is not Iraq. Misery comes in many forms. Afghanistan has a more impossible border, but it does have some positives. The majority of the population is in the north and west and is supportive. One thing Mr Smith might do is encourage them to be also rewarded. The north and west is neglected by the Karzai government, which plays Pashtun politics in the south and east. This is a mistake. In both Afghanistan and Pakistan, it is not a bad idea to think of them regionally as well as nationally. Strengthening stable regions at least limits fundamentalist penetration. Mr Smith will also note that local resentment in Afghanistan is nothing like that in Iraq. Afghans regard themselves as having a major hand in their liberation, both from the Taliban and earlier the Russians. Aid, they feel, is no more than their due, and they have a disposition to welcome their allies. Afghanistan is not a conquered and occupied nation.[115]

Even more bullishly, retired Australian General Jim Molan was quoted in late 2008 as saying:

> The Afghanistan war is winnable. We are not being asked to do the impossible. It is not going any worse than just about any other war. No wars go well initially and the average length of a counter-insurgency is 9 years. We are really in only the second year and, just as we did not get serious about the Iraq war until its fifth year, we are not yet serious about the Afghan war.[116]

Australian expert opinion on Afghanistan in the news media has therefore struck a very different note than its counterpart in Britain. Where British experts have often stressed the unwinnability of the war, Australians have insisted that the situation, though grave, is not hopeless. Australian experts have also stressed the high importance of prevailing in Afghanistan, unlike many British experts such as Stewart who have claimed that there are other cheaper ways to attain Western goals. In short, Australia has seen remarkably little elite discord over the war in Afghanistan—such discord cannot, therefore, explain the trajectory of public opinion.

Multilateralism. The paucity of opinion polls on the Afghanistan issue in Australia makes it hard to assess the impact of a lack of multilateral burden-sharing on support for the war. Certainly the deployment by Nicholas Sarkozy of additional French troops does not appear to have moved support in Australia one way or the other.

Australia is, numerically, one of the lower contributing nations in our analysis. If the share of the burden is an important factor, we should then see higher support in Australia than elsewhere, and we should see support in Australia fall when additional troops are sent to bolster those currently deployed.

We do see somewhat stronger support in Australia than in Canada or Britain, though weaker than in the United States, which has contributed most of all. Moreover, many other theories would also suggest we would see support hold up longer in Australia than elsewhere. At the same time, since the Rudd Government deployed an additional 450 troops to Afghanistan in April 2009,[117] this should have caused public support to drop. Opinion polls have revealed that a plurality of Australians opposes this move, but there is no evidence to suggest it has caused support for the entire deployment to fall.[118] Moreover, there are many other potential explanations for this result. There is, in short, little evidence that a lack of multilateral burden sharing accounts for much of the fall in support in the Australian case.

Principal Policy Objective. The shift in principal policy objective from restraint to counterinsurgency does not seem to have had much of an impact in Australia. Although it is difficult to be sure because we do not know what level of support the war commanded in Australia when the initial invasion was launched, the critical drop in public support does not seem to begin until 2007, long after the principal policy objective had clearly switched from foreign policy restraint to counterinsurgency. This case therefore suggests that if casualties remain low and the political and news media elite remain behind the mission and publicly confident of its success, then the public can be persuaded to put aside their misgivings about a counterinsurgency operation, at least initially.

Prospects for Success. At first glance, the Australian case seems problematic for the idea that the mission's diminishing prospects for success explain the fall in support. After all, if the Australian elite are still maintaining that victory is achievable and casualties are still low, why has public support been falling?

The answer to this is twofold. First, although the Australian elite have maintained a consensus that the war is winnable, they are by no means starry-eyed optimists about victory. Rather, Kilcullen, Evans, and others have made clear that there is a very real risk of defeat, and that it is increasing by the day.

Second, even if Australia's political and military elite were united in a rosily optimistic view of the Afghan conflict, Australians are still subjected to the same news coming out of Afghanistan as other countries. The Australian news media report the resurgence of the Taliban,[119] the growing doubts about the war in Europe and North America,[120] the casualties suffered by other militaries,[121] and the misgivings expressed by experts in other countries, especially in Britain,[122] whose ties with Australia are still very close. Thus, Australians are hardly insulated from the bad news about Afghanistan even if their own elite are still broadly in favor of the war.

Moreover, Australia is the toughest case for the theory that the progress of the war on the ground is the key factor. All other factors would point towards support remaining high. Australian casualties are simply too low for a purely casualty-based explanation to make sense. Australia has the most united elite of any participating country except the United States. The Australian public is not generally anti-American, or broadly unused to or opposed to military intervention overseas. Australia is shouldering a relatively small share of the burden compared to its major allies. The fact that, in spite of all these factors, public support for the war has dropped below majority levels is strong evidence that the progress of the war on the ground is the most important determinant of public support for the war—the factor that can, in fact, trump all others.

Afghanistan-Specific Theories.

Iraq. Australia, along with the United States, is a very useful case to gauge the extent to which negative spillovers from Iraq have damaged support for the war in Afghanistan. Recall that if participation in the Iraq war is said to destroy the foreign policy credibility of the incumbent so that all of his policies become tainted by association, then opponents of the Iraq war's credibility should rise and their policies will be more readily accepted. Thus if a pro-Iraq war leader is replaced by an anti-Iraq but pro-Afghanistan war leader, support for the Afghanistan war should rise.

This is precisely what happened in 2007 when the anti-Iraq war Labor Party assumed power in Canberra. The new Prime Minister Kevin Rudd swiftly withdrew Australian troops from Iraq, but maintained and in fact increased their numbers in Afghanistan.[123] If the Iraq war really was a major factor behind the drop in support for the war in Afghanistan, we should have expected to see Australian support for the latter war increase under Rudd. Instead, the very opposite has happened, as the polls outlined in the introductory section make clear. In Australia, then, as in the United States, the Iraq war is simply not a key factor in explaining why public support for the Afghanistan war has fallen.

Confused Rationale. In common with other countries, many Australians have cited the confused and shifting rationales used by politicians as a key factor in the decline of support. For example, Daniel Cotterill, former Chief of Staff to Defense Minister Joel Fitzgibbons, stated:

> It is very likely that Rudd will agree to any request from President Obama for Australia to boost our military commitment in Afghanistan, but it is just as likely that he will remain unable to clearly define our war aims, outline what will constitute victory or give any idea of how long that will take. Australian soldiers are doing a great job in Afghanistan, but unless we are content for them to stay there indefinitely our politicians and our policymakers need to lift their game.[124]

Support for this may be found in the Lowy Institute's poll of 2008, in which only 50 percent of respondents said they were confident that the Australian Government has "clear goals" in Afghanistan. Moreover, 80 percent of those who did say that Australia has clear goals supported continued involvement, while 86 percent of those who said Australia did not have clear goals opposed continued involvement.[125]

Yet when one examines the statements of Australian leaders of both Liberal and Labor Governments, it is striking how closely they stick to one clear overarching war aim. Both have, overwhelmingly, stressed the counterterrorism-security rationale to the exclusion of arguments about nation-building, women's rights, or the drug trade. For example, in announcing further reinforcements in April 2006, Liberal Defense Minister Brendan Nelson stated:

> Australians need to appreciate that fighting terrorism is a global activity and we are not going to wait for these people to turn up on Australian beaches, so to speak.[126]

On a visit to Australian troops in Uruzgan Province, Prime Minister Howard stated:

> Our troops in Afghanistan are doing very valuable but very dangerous work. Each deployment involves a very important struggle against terrorism.[127]

Again in an interview with the Nine News Network, Howard continued to stress the sole overriding reason for the deployment was counterterrorism, with nation-building a subordinate means to that end:

> I can't give a date. It will only end when we and our allies are certain that the terrorists won't have a safe haven in Afghanistan and when we are reasonably satisfied that the democratically elected government of that country can exert its authority and it's responsible for

> us to go. It is long. It is difficult. I can understand people asking those questions. There is a lot at stake because if we lose in Afghanistan and the terrorists get a safe haven there, that is a direct threat of instability in our own region and, of course, a very great concern to Australia. Bear in mind we are dealing with an organization that was the inspiration for the Bali attack (in 2002) that killed 88 Australians, so it is not some distant, far away conflict in which we have no concern and no responsibility.[128]

Again, in response to the death of an SAS trooper, Howard stated:

> It's not going to alter the attitude of the government towards the commitment in Afghanistan. It is very important we contain terrorism in that country, it is very important we contain terrorism in Iraq. The worst thing this country could do is to say it is all too hard and to give up and retreat into our own shell imagining it would make the problem go away.[129]

In the earliest years of the insurgency, Howard's rhetoric was somewhat less disciplined, relying on more general and abstract formulations about defending the Australian way of life:

> The struggle against terrorism in which this country is engaged is not going to end soon. It will go on for some time. It will require a great deal of persistence. There will be times when people will wonder whether it is worth the effort. But let me say to you that it is worth the effort because the sort of way of life that we are opposing is a way of life that would never win any acceptance in our country, it's a way of life which is completely anathema to everything that this country stands for.[130]

Nonetheless, it is undeniable that the Howard Government's public rationales for the war were far more tightly drawn than those of many other Governments.

Moreover, Howard's rhetorical focus on the terrorism rationale was carried on by his successor Kevin Rudd. Speaking as Leader of the Opposition shortly prior to the election, Rudd claimed:

> What we've got there is Osama bin Laden and al Qaeda, the original terrorists responsible for September 11. It's also the area which provided the training for those who engaged in the bombings in Bali which killed nearly 100 Australians. And for those reasons it's a military campaign which we need to prosecute to the end.[131]

Following his election, Rudd continued to portray Australian involvement in Afghanistan in terms of counterterrorism. Terming the war a mission of "strategic denial of an operational base for international terrorist organizations," Rudd stated: "I take the mission of strategic denial very seriously. We must remain resolved in the execution of that mission of strategic denial."[132]

Elaborating further, Rudd reminded Australians of the original reasons for the deployment:

> We are there because a failed state was giving open succor and support to a global terrorist organization, al-Qa'ida, which then attacked our ally the U.S. on September 11, 2001, and in the process murdered 3000 people. We, as a consequence of our alliance with the US, embarked upon a combined military action with them. Nothing has changed since then.[133]

Rudd's language in this passage may suggest a depiction of the Afghan operation as being undertaken to help Australia's ally, the United States. Yet, as Opposition Foreign Affairs spokesman, he had criticized John Howard for joining the war in Iraq when he believed the real threat to Australia's security came from Afghanistan:

> Our call on John Howard is to make sure Australia's national security resources are delivered toward the elimination of al Qaeda root and branch in Afghanistan because that's where they intend to do our people harm from.[134]

Kevin Rudd has, in short, followed John Howard in communicating consistently to the Australian people over many years that the strategic aim of the Australian deployment is counterterrorism.

So why do so many Australians feel they are not clear about the objectives of the war? Here it may be useful to distinguish between communicating a clear aim and communicating a clear operational plan to achieve that aim. It would be hard to see how Australians could be unclear on the broader strategic aim of the war, yet it is entirely possible that they could be clear on the broader aim but unclear on the specifics of how to get there. Too often proponents of the "lack of a clear rationale" explanation confuse the two. The problem with Rudd characterizing the mission as one of "strategic denial" is that it is very unclear how and when, if ever, the territory of Afghanistan could be permanently denied to al-Qaeda. As Jentleson would point out, it is far easier for voters to conceive of how to win a Gulf War type operation. If, on the other hand, voters cannot even clearly picture what a victory would look like, it is evident that they will not believe that the war is winnable. It is this, more than a lack of clarity about the war's overarching aim, that most likely lies behind complaints in Australia about a lack of clear objectives.

Conclusion. The Australian case suffers from some missing data, but, nonetheless, it is very instructive. As with the United States, casualties are not the only factor—otherwise Australian support would fall as much as it apparently has, unless one were to argue that Australia is inherently more casualty sensitive than other participating nations such as Canada, but this seems unlikely. Elite discord also cannot be cited as a key factor. Australian support for the war has fallen substantially in spite of a relatively united elite in favor of the war, both inside and outside Parliament. Similarly, the fall in support came after the switch in the principal policy objective—suggesting Australian voters are not strictly averse to counterinsurgency campaigns, provided they believe they still have a good shot at success. Likewise, pinning the blame on confused and shifting rationales does not explain the trajectory of Australian support, at least if the confusion refers only to the broader strategic aim of the mission. In fact, Australian leaders have been comparatively tight and focused in their elaboration of the reason for the war. If confusion exists among the Australian people, it is more likely to revolve around the criteria by which one may judge victory to have been accomplished.

This explanation, however, fits well with the claim that the progress of the war on the ground is the key factor. In fact, the Australian case is perhaps the best evidence in this study that prospects for victory is the key. For all other factors which the literature has identified as important in determining public support for a war are trending in favor of public support holding firm. Only the situation in Afghanistan itself, which is common to Australia and the other participating nations, could be pushing popular support down. To be sure, support does not appear to have dropped quite so much in Australia as in some other places (though the polling evidence is somewhat shaky), and this suggests that the other factors have some purchase over the Australian case (for example, if the Australian elite were more divided or the rationales had been more confusing or casualties had been higher, support would probably have dropped further). Nonetheless, the diminishing prospects for victory are the strongest factors driving Australian support down.

BACK ON AFGHANISTAN'S PLAINS—PUBLIC SUPPORT FOR THE AFGHAN WAR IN BRITAIN

Of all of the countries under study, Britain has a strong claim to be historically the most enthusiastic for overseas intervention. Britain is, of course, a former imperial power, which ruled over the Indian subcontinent and intervened in Afghanistan three times in the 19th and early 20th centuries. Britain's involvement with the country was not a happy one, however, and led to a humiliating defeat in the 1840s when the British expeditionary force in Afghanistan was wiped out to the last man.[135] Tending to forget the victorious outcome to the 1878 intervention, Britain's historical memory of Afghanistan is of a very difficult and dangerous military assignment, exemplified in Rudyard Kipling's famous poem, "The Young British Soldier," in which a sergeant advises a young recruit "when you're rolling around on Afghanistan's plains/ and the women come out to carve up what remains/ just roll on your rifle and blow out your brains/ and go to your God like a soldier."[136] As we shall see, this popular folk memory of Afghanistan has frequently been used by British opponents of the war.

Over the course of a long decolonization, Britain fought numerous small counterinsurgency wars—Malaya, Borneo, Aden, Kenya, and Cyprus.[137] Britain also endured a 25 plus-year insurgency with the Irish Republican Army (IRA) in Northern Ireland, claiming well over 1,000 British military and police casualties, plus many civilians.[138] The British also fought regular conventional wars in the Falklands against Argentina[139] and played a major role in Operation DESERT STORM.[140] Although Prime Minister Tony Blair was elected promising a "new Britain" shorn of many of the old imperial trappings,[141] Blair in fact proved even more willing than his Conservative predecessors to use force overseas. Under Blair's watch, even before 9/11, British troops or airmen were engaged in action in Kosovo, in Iraq for Operation DESERT FOX in 1998, in a successful peace enforcement operation in Sierra Leone, and in peacekeeping missions in Macedonia and East Timor.[142] Consequently, the British public exhibited a great deal of ease with the deployment of British forces overseas and with the use of force in international affairs. In a Pew Global Research poll of 2004, 67 percent of British respondents believed that the use of force to maintain order in international affairs is legitimate, fully 46 percent higher than the corresponding figure in Germany.[143] Opinion polls on Bosnia and Kosovo revealed a ready willingness on the part of the British public to resort to force. Polls indicated that 54 percent of the British public supported the use of ground forces to remove Serbian forces from Kosovo—higher than the U.S. figure and higher than in any other European Union (EU) member state except for France.[144] Throughout the crisis, support for the NATO campaign never dropped below 50 percent in Britain and ended over 60 percent.[145] In the previous Bosnian operations, 59 percent of British respondents expressed support for airstrikes against the Bosnian Serbs in 1995 and public support for the British deployment in the country wavered between 62 percent and 74 percent. Only 32 percent of British respondents in the same polls claimed to want a pullout in the event of British casualties.[146]

Relations with the United States are often couched in terms of the "special relationship" and Churchillian rhetoric about the bonds between the English-speaking nations solidified by shared experiences in the two world wars. Yet the clichés do bear a reasonable degree of accuracy in describing a reasonable degree of closeness between the two countries. Attitudes towards the United States in Great Britain are the most positive of all the major EU nations. In 2004, the BBC and many other broadcasters carried out a survey of attitudes towards the United States in 11 countries in various areas of the world. British respondents gave the United States a net favorability rating of 75 percent, against a sample average of 54 percent, and a French score of 41 percent net favorable. A net percentage of 56 percent of Britons also agreed that the United States is a force for good in the world, against 35 percent in France, while only 33 percent net agreed that "the United States scares me."[147] Pew Global's polling revealed similar attitudes. The United States began the 21st century with a favorability rating in Britain of 83 percent, higher than in any other major EU nation. Even by the end of the Bush Presidency, a majority of Britons (53 percent) still had a positive view of the United States.[148] The UK does, however, exhibit certain strains of anti-Americanism, which it is important not to overlook—only a slight majority of Britons believed that al Qaeda was behind 9/11 (although 5 percent blamed the U.S. Government itself).[149] Moreover, the BBC poll revealed that 51 percent of Britons believed that "the United States is reaping the thorns planted by its rulers in the world," though this figure is far lower than the corresponding one for France—76 percent.[150] In all, then, although Britain in the period we are studying was not free of anti-Americanism, it is one of the most pro-American nations in Europe and the world. Overtly anti-American arguments against the Afghan war would be falling on difficult ground.

Undoubtedly confident of firm backing from the British people, Blair committed British troops from the beginning of Operation Enduring Freedom—initially Special Forces from the SAS and Special Boat Service (SBS), later Royal Marines, and finally "county" infantry regiments along with the Provincial Reconstruction Teams after the initial stages of the fighting had died down. Since the resurgence of the Taliban in 2005, the British have especially borne a heavy burden in the increased fighting; 239 British troops have died in Afghanistan since 2001.[151] Public support, over the same period, has dropped from initial highs of 73 percent[152] to current levels of 37 percent,[153] though support has been even lower.

What accounts for this drastic reduction in support?

Casualties.

Logarithmic Casualties. Gaps in British polling data make it hard to tell whether the arc of support has followed a Mueller-style logarithmic decline. As we can see by looking at Figure 8, support began high and has since dropped considerably, but there is a long polling gap between 2001 and 2006 when Afghanistan fell off the political radar in the UK and was eclipsed by the (at the time) far more controversial Iraq war. Only the resurgence of the Taliban in 2006 and the resumption of British casualties turned British news media attention back to central Asia. Once polling resumed in 2006, public opinion had turned from majority support to majority opposition, but we have no idea when the switch occurred or how sudden it was. Since 2006, support has flatlined at a level just below 40 percent, although at times it has dropped below 30 percent, albeit only briefly and slightly. The flatlining could just about be considered consistent with a logarithmic model, as it predicts that support will fall off more gradually after an initial sharp drop. However, the actual pattern since 2006, as shown in Figure 9, is better described as fluctuating significantly around the mid 30% level, rather than sedately declining. Thus, one can tentatively conclude that the British data do not fit a logarithmic pattern. Does the data follow another purely casualty-driven pattern?

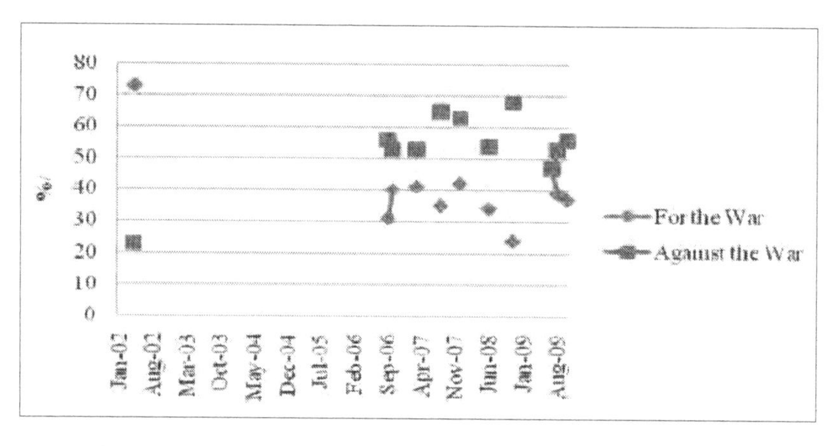

Figure 8. UK Public Opinion and the War in Afghanistan, 2002-09.

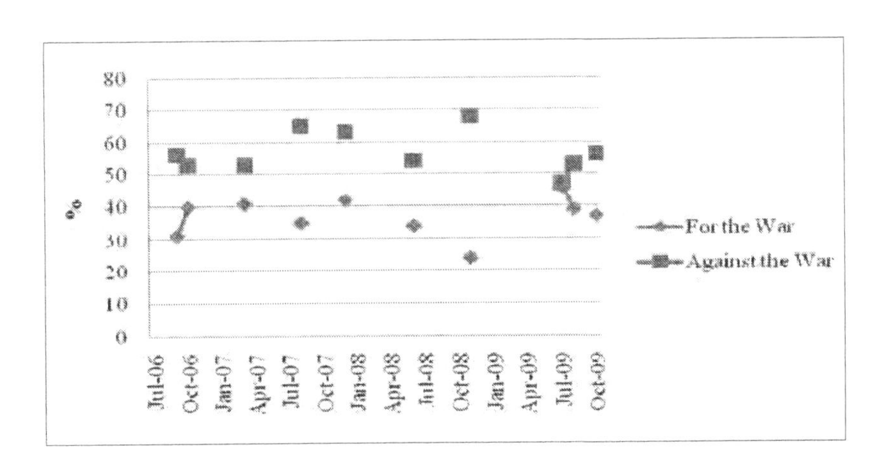

Figure 9. UK Public Opinion and the War in Afghanistan, 2006-09.

Marginal Casualties. Gauging the impact of marginal casualties by eye is a much easier task when casualties can be seen on the same timeline as public support. If public opinion responds simply and directly to the latest casualty "shock," then upward spikes in casualties should be swiftly followed by downward spikes in support. This is not, however, essentially what we see (see Figures 10 and 11).

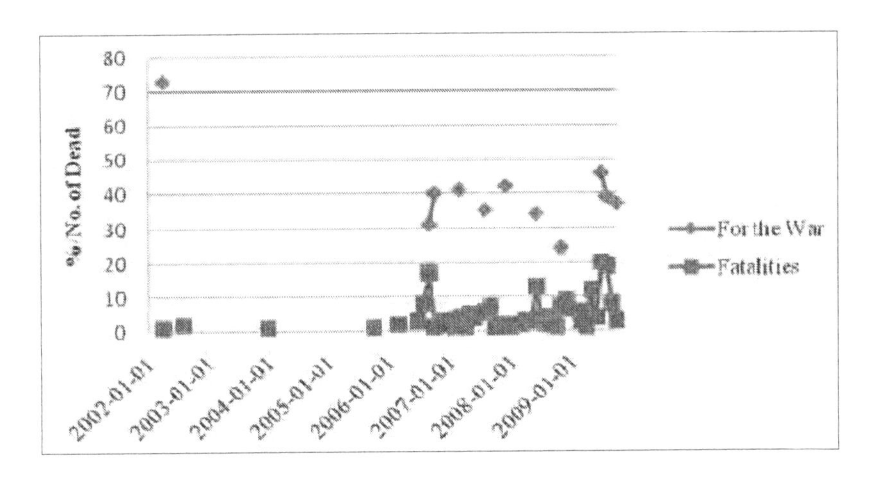

Figure 10. UK Support for the War and Fatalities, 2002-09.

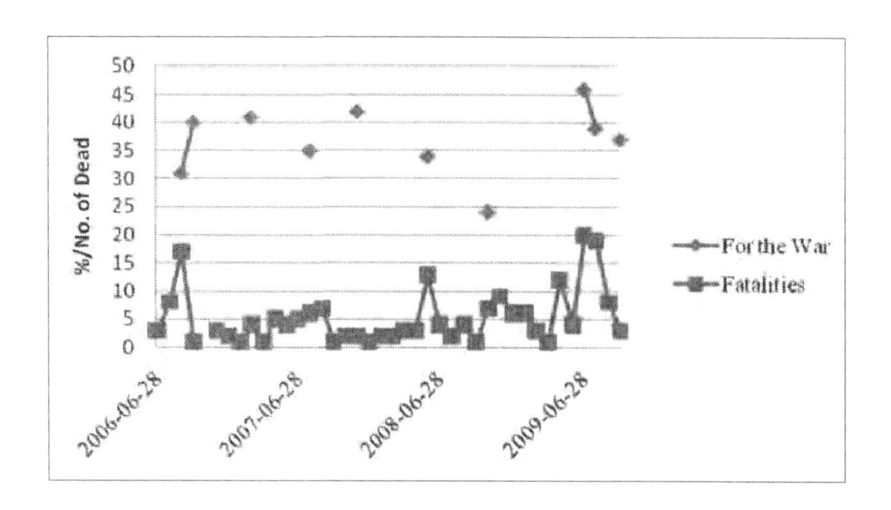

Figure 11. UK Support for the War and Fatalities, 2006-09.

In fact, spikes in British casualties in September 2006 are immediately followed by a slight increase in support for the war. A sharp drop between December 2007 and June 2008 coincides with a period of steady but relatively low casualties. It is true that the summer of 2008 saw a further sharp drop after a very bloody period of fighting, but this drop had in fact begun over the quieter winter period. Finally, opinion polls taken after the recent British casualties in Helmand—nine dead in 1 day, the worst British loss of life in combat on 1 day since 2001—appears to have precipitated an increase in support, according to the latest BBC/ICM Poll.

Although plagued with gaps, the data on British public opinion and the Afghanistan war show that British public opinion, like its American and Australian counterpart, is not reflexively determined by casualties alone. Other factors also come into play.

Casualties Plus Politics.

Elite Consensus. According to Eric Larsson's original formulation, Britain, in fact, exhibited a high degree of political consensus in favor of the war throughout the period in question. All three major nationwide parties have supported the war throughout the period in question. Even the Liberal Democrats, opponents of the Iraq war and the most wary of all three parties about the use of force overseas, have supported the British mission. Recently, the Brown Government has faced criticism from the Conservatives and the Liberal Democrats about its handling of the war—specifically underfunding the British military and failing to provide the equipment, especially helicopters, which they believe are needed in Afghanistan.[154] However, neither Leader of the Opposition David Cameron nor the Liberal Democract leader Nick Clegg have advocated withdrawing from Afghanistan.[155] Parliamentary opposition to the war has concentrated around maverick leftwingers in the Labour Party such as Paul Flynn and Michael Meacher,[156] and George Galloway of the self-founded anti-war Respect Party.[157] However, such figures are far from the center of power. Recently some figures closer to the political center, such as former Minister Kim Howells MP, have spoken out against the war—but this came long after the main drop in public support had occurred.[158]

Yet this does not mean that Britain has truly seen an "elite" consensus as outlined in the introduction. For a large number of figures in the press, many traditionally conservative in most issues, have long been skeptical of British involvement in Afghanistan and have grown louder as the mission has floundered. Within the broadsheet press, both leftists such as *The Indepen-*

dent's Robert Fisk,[159] and conservative "realists" such as Sir Michael Howard,[160] the (conservative) *Times'* Simon Jenkins[161] and Matthew Parris,[162] have fiercely criticized British involvement, advocated withdrawal, and seized on any reverses for the NATO operation. They have recently been joined by other news media figures such as the famous war correspondent and former editor of the *Daily Telegraph*, Max Hastings,[163] and the British author and diplomat Rory Stewart.[164] In a situation unparalleled in any other country under study, even serving diplomats and soldiers have voiced their doubts about the mission. The British Ambassador to Kabul, Sir Sherard Cowper-Coles, was quoted as saying that the American strategy in Afghanistan is "doomed to fail."[165] Shortly thereafter, one of the most senior British military officers in Afghanistan, Brigadier Mark Carleton-Smith of the 16th Air Assault Brigade, said that a military victory over the Taliban was neither "feasible nor supportable."[166] Of course, Carleton-Smith was attempting to make a subtle argument that military force would have to be supplemented by political progress (including talks with the Taliban) and could not be expected to bring the war to a satisfactory conclusion alone,[167] while Cowper-Coles' employers at the Foreign Office insisted that his comments were "exaggerated."[168] Yet, public opinion often has little time for such intricacies and would be most likely to deduce from these comments that the professionals on the ground were concluding that the war was unwinnable and a British withdrawal was the best course of action.

In fact, such a broad-based movement against the war among so many knowledgeable and ostensibly nonpartisan figures in the news media and public service may be more debilitating than a straightforward partisan split. Men such as Hastings or Stewart (a former Army officer who served in a senior position in the British occupation authorities in Iraq and has travelled widely within Afghanistan[169]) are more knowledgeable about the region and may carry more clout with the general public in Britain than the various figures in the Labour Government who have sought to defend the intervention. Moreover, their criticisms have centered on the prospects for success of the operation, and they have used their detailed knowledge of the area to argue that the current strategy will not work and that British interests and Western security may be better served by other strategies, such as co-opting moderate Taliban or working through warlord proxies. Opponents of the Afghan war have also frequently invoked Britain's Victorian reversals in the country to argue that Afghanistan is inherently impossible to pacify—"has the British Army learnt nothing?" asked Simon Jenkins rhetorically.[170] In early 2009, Guardian cartoonist Steve Bell depicted President Barack Obama in the pith helmet and red tunic of Queen Victoria's Army, riding towards the Khyber Pass while a wizened George W. Bush by the roadside recites Kipling's famous poem as a warning.[171]

More prosaically, in terms of the cost-benefit analysis outlined by Gelpi and Feaver, Stewart, and others have argued both that the prospects for success are low and that the benefits of success, even were they to be attained, are much lower than the British leadership claims:

> Even if—as seems most unlikely—the Taliban was to take the capital, it is not clear how much of a threat this would pose to U.S. or European national security. Would it repeat its error of providing a safe haven to al Qaeda? And how safe would this haven be? And does

> al Qaeda still require large terrorist training camps to organise attacks? Could it not plan in Hamburg and train at flight schools in Florida; or meet in Bradford and build morale on an adventure training course in Wales? Furthermore, there are no self-evident connections between the key objectives of counter-terrorism, development, democracy, state-building and counter-insurgency. Counter-insurgency is neither a necessary nor a sufficient condition for state-building. You could create a stable legitimate state without winning a counter-insurgency campaign (India, which is far more stable and legitimate than Afghanistan, is still fighting several long counter-insurgency campaigns from Assam to Kashmir). You could win a counter-insurgency campaign without creating a stable state (if such a state also required the rule of law and a legitimate domestic economy). Nor is there any necessary connection between state-formation and terrorism. Our confusions are well illustrated by the debates about whether Iraq was a rogue state harboring terrorists (as Bush claimed) or an authoritarian state that excluded terrorists (as was the case).[172]

Whether one accepts the claims of Stewart or other British opponents of the war, it is difficult for supporters of the war to argue that he and his colleagues do not know what they are talking about, or that they are extreme leftists, anti-Americans, or party hacks. Proof of a specific link between the news media activism of British "realist" opponents of the war and the frequent leaks from the military and diplomatic service suggesting that their concerns are shared by many of Britain's senior soldiers and diplomats will be discussed below. Especially, it will be argued that highly informed elite British critics of the war have very successfully undermined public support by creating a large degree of doubt about the prospective success of the mission. The interaction between casualties, elite dissensus in the news media and government, and diminishing prospects for success appear to be the key drivers of the fall in support in Britain.

Principal Policy Objective. Lack of data makes it hard to determine the independent effect of the switch from a restraint to a counterinsurgency mission. To gauge such an effect, we should see British support beginning high in 2001-02 but drop sharply when it becomes clear that a prolonged counterinsurgency is in prospect. This is indeed what we see, with a drop below majority levels at the start of the insurgency in 2006. However, Afghanistan had clearly moved from a restraint mission many years before then, but we do not have any polls for this period to determine what effect this shift had.

Multilateralism. A lack of multilateral burden sharing does not seem to have had a major effect on the trajectory of British support. This can be seen by examining British reaction to Sarkozy's deployment of additional French troops in the spring of 2008. During this time, as the previous figures show, British support for the war underwent a sharp decline. There was no noticeable effect of more equitable burden sharing on the trajectory of British opinion about the war, unless in some way greater French participation could be expected to reduce support for the war.

Prospects for Success. Close examination of the British case reveals strong evidence for the crucial effect of the progress of the war on the ground. For a start, it may be argued that the lack of polling data from 2002 to 2006 itself is a significant "dog which did not bark." For it may suggest that the British public and news media believed the Afghan war to have been essentially won, and therefore no longer controversial. For example, a *London Times* leader of December 2004, following the Afghan election, stated:

> Many of those bereaved on September 11, 2001, may still be asking themselves if anything unequivocally good can come of that day. The swearing-in yesterday of Hamid Karzai as President of Afghanistan offered a positive answer. As a direct result of the attacks on New York and Washington, Afghanistan has, for the first time, a democratically-elected leader who is respected at home and abroad, and fiercely committed to weaning his country off warlordism and the opium poppy. For the first time, likewise, Afghanistan has the rest of the world on its side. The international community is now heavily invested in what was the definitive failed state, and too grimly aware of how that failure was exploited by extremists.[173]

It is also significant that when, in June 2005, 400 additional British troops were deployed to take command of the International Security Assistance Force (ISAF) in Kabul, their deployment merited a mere 94-word article on page 9 of the *London Times*.[174]

Thus the resurgence of the Taliban in late 2005 and early 2006 not only surprised public opinion and the news media in the West, but caused them to rapidly revise their estimate of the prospects of success for the war—from already won to potentially loseable. *The Independent* concluded in September 2006:

> *It is now apparent that the battle for Afghanistan did not end in 2001.* The fall of Kabul was merely the beginning of that struggle. And, as this latest murder shows, the terrible truth is that *the forces of enlightenment and democracy are in retreat.*[175]

Significantly for the prospects for success thesis, September 2006 saw the first British polls to reveal majority opposition to the war, when Britain had suffered only a few casualties.

Moreover, drops in British public support for the war track rather well with pessimistic assessments of the situation on the ground. The month after Cowper-Coles' and Carleton-Smith's comments were reported in the British press, public support fell to its lowest level of the entire campaign—24 percent.[176] The previous few months were not, however, notably bad in terms of casualties—only seven British troops lost their lives in the preceding 3 months, versus seven, nine, and six in the 3 following months.

One interpretation of the trajectory of British public support, then, is that the majority of the casualty-phobes and defeat-phobes in the British public were "burned off" by the news from Afghanistan in late 2006 and early 2007. Yet this would also happen if casualties alone were the key factor. What remains puzzling is why British support for the war, having fallen to the mid 30 percent level, then stabilized.

As can be seen from the figures, British support for the war fell in late 2006 to below majority levels, but it has essentially remained at that same level since then, fluctuating around the 35 percent to 40 percent marks. This suggests that the Feaver-Gelpi model of a contingent of hard-core hawks comprising around a third of the population, who will continue to support a mission with very little sensitivity to casualties, fits the British case rather well. Over 85 percent of Britain's casualties have been incurred since September 2006, but public support for the war has not dropped significantly further since. More difficult for the prospects for success theory to explain are the recent polls showing that support for the British mission rose to its highest levels since 2006 in the early summer of 2009, even in the direct aftermath of the nine fatalities in Operation PANTHER'S CLAW in Helmand.

Although different polls for the BBC and ITN gave widely differing results (ITN still showing majority opposition, the BBC showing an almost even split),[177] both showed support to have risen since its nadir in November 2008 and to be at the very least comparable with the levels last seen in 2006 and 2007. Recent Angus Reid polls suggest that the ITN figures were closer to the mark,[178] but this would still represent a stabilizing, if not a recovery, of support for the war. It seems that the hard-core hawks have remained solid on the war.

Moreover, the most recent polls from September and October represent a return to the status quo ante of support in the mid-30 percentages, suggesting the brief stabilization of support earlier in the year may have been little more than noise in the data. This comes hard on the heels of the same news that has affected American public opinion—especially the summer election, which in addition to the fraud allegations saw minimal turnout in the areas of Helmand province, the low turnout in Helmand, which the British Army had fought so hard to secure during Operation PANTHER'S CLAW,[179] was seen by many as indicative of a wasted sacrifice and a failing war effort. That support did not plummet in the UK over the summer as it did in the United States may be due only to the fact that it was already so low that it had little room to fall.

Afghanistan-Specific Theories.

Confused Rationales. It is not surprising that British analysts should be among the most enthusiastic proponents of the case that confused rationales have hampered support for the operation. The reasons given for the Afghanistan deployment between 2006 and 2009 by the British Government were seen by some as a prime example of how *not* to rally support for a war. In a speech to the House of Commons announcing the deployment of 3,300 additional British troops to Helmand Province, which marked the beginning of the current phase of Britain's Afghanistan War, Defense Secretary John Reid gave three different reasons for the British deployment—anti-terrorism, counter-narcotics, and development.

> Last September, I visited Afghanistan. I saw for myself the real hope that the International Community has brought to a new generation of Afghans. The hope that at last the Afghan people can rebuild their country. The hope that Afghanistan can take its rightful place as a country where men and women, both of them, can live in peace and freedom with real hope for a better future. We cannot risk losing those achievements. We cannot risk Afghanistan once again becoming a sanctuary for terrorists—we have seen where that leads, be it in New York or here in London. We cannot ignore the opportunity to bring security to a fragile but vital part of the world. And we cannot go on accepting Afghan opium being the source of ninety per cent of the heroin which is applied to the veins of the young people of our country. For all these reasons, it is in our interests, as the UK, and as a responsible member of the international community, to act.[180]

However, in a subsequent visit to British forces in Afghanistan widely reported in the British news media, Reid gave what was widely interpreted as a confusing statement to the press. Attempting to stress that the British were primarily in Helmand for reconstruction, but would fight back if attacked by the Taliban or al Qaeda, Reid stated:

> Although our mission to Afghanistan is primarily reconstruction it is a dangerous mission because the terrorists will want to destroy the economy and the legitimate trade the Government has built up. . . . Of course, our primary mission is not counter-terrorism but one of the tasks we will have to perform will be to defend our own troops.[181]

In a quote that has become infamous in British politics, Reid went on to say that he would be happy if British troops completed their mission "without a shot being fired."[182] Reid's successor as Defense Secretary, Des Browne, continued in the same vein as his predecessor. Announcing the deployment of additional British troops to Afghanistan, Browne gave a purely humanitarian rationale:

> NATO must respond to this request, or we will put at risk everything we have achieved across Afghanistan in the last five years: the stability which has brought five million refugees home, the advances in democracy, the economy, human rights and women's rights.[183]

In contradiction to Reid's previous statement, Browne went on to state that British forces are not "a counternarcotics police."[184]

This rhetorical strategy accompanied the decline of public support for the war between 2006 and 2008. Moreover Reid's statements on Afghanistan date from early 2006, before it became clear that public support had dropped in Britain. He was not motivated to try shifting rationales by concerns about the failure of the rationales he had previously been using—because it was not clear to him at that stage that they actually had failed.

However, at the beginning of 2009, the British Government began to change tack. Believing in the damaging effect that shifting rationales were having on public support for the British deployment, Prime Minister Brown, his Foreign Secretary David Milliband, and Defence Secretary Bob Ainsworth have sought to justify the British deployment purely in terms of security. As Prime Minister Brown himself stated:

> Eight years ago, after September 11th 2001, the case for intervention in Afghanistan was clear: to remove the Taleban regime and deprive al Qaeda of a safe base for terrorist plots that were a threat to countries across the world.
>
> In 2009, the case for our continued involvement is the same—to prevent terrorist attacks here in Britain and across the world by dealing with the threat at its source: that crucible of terror on the border and mountain areas of Afghanistan and Pakistan.
>
> We must not forget that three-quarters of terror plots against the UK have roots in these areas.[185]

Similarly, Foreign Secretary Milliband claimed in an interview with the *Times*:

> We must ensure that Afghanistan cannot again become an incubator for terrorism and a launching pad for attacks on us.
>
> This is about the future of Britain because we know that the borderlands of Afghanistan and Pakistan have been used to launch terrible attacks, not just on the U.S. but on Britain as well.[186]

Again, in the House of Commons, debate called after the nine British deaths in Operation PANTHER'S CLAW, Milliband heavily stressed an exclusively security-based rationale:

> The defining mission in Afghanistan is simply stated: to ensure that, with al Qaeda having been driven out of Afghanistan, it cannot come back under the safe umbrella of renewed Taliban rule.[187]

Even Shadow Foreign Secretary, the Conservative MP William Hague, admitted that a far clearer line had emerged on Afghanistan from the Brown Government in 2009:

> It is vital, too, that we are clear about what we are trying to do, and the Foreign Secretary was clear about that in his speech. We went into Afghanistan not out of choice, but out of necessity—to deny al Qaeda the use of Afghanistan as a launch pad for training and planning attacks on Western targets. It was a collective national purpose that was accepted by all parts of the House, and the consequences of failure are so serious for the whole region and the wider world that we have to do our utmost to make it work. *So, although there have been what my right hon. Friend the Leader of the Opposition described yesterday as sometimes "lofty" and "vague" objectives over recent years, the Foreign Secretary has moved the Government towards defining our objectives in a more tightly drawn fashion.*[188]

However, having first adopted a more disciplined rhetorical strategy, Brown reverted to a plethora of rationales later in the year, as evidenced by his speech to the International Institute for Strategic Studies:

- Continuing the enhancement of security for our forces
- Expanding the vital work that has discovered and dismantled 1000 IEDs this summer
- A radical step-up in the training of Afghan forces -
- Britain ready to work with allies to train around 10,000 new forces in Helmand alone
- Stronger district governors in Helmand and across Afghanistan's 400 districts
- Local communities empowered to run their own affairs

- Backed up by a civilian strategy to provide clean policing and services as well as security
- Through our development work, securing for Afghans a greater economic stake in the future of their country.
- And pressure on the new government for an anti-corruption drive throughout the country

> These are aims that are clear and justified—and also realistic and achievable. It remains my judgment that a safer Britain requires a safer Afghanistan and in Afghanistan last week, I was further convinced that, despite the challenges we face, a nation emerging from three decades of violence can be healed and strengthened; and that our country and the whole world can be safer; because together we have the values, the strategy and the resolve to complete our vital task.[189]

Britain is one case in which the confused and shifting rationales offered by political leaders seem to have undoubtedly played an important role. In spite of Brown's personal unpopularity, the switch to a more focused rhetorical strategy did lead to something of a revival in support in mid-2009, one which, however, Brown then himself undid by returning to the multiple rationales used by Reid and others in the past.

Conclusion. Many factors have brought about the decline in British support. Singling one out above the others is problematic. First, casualties alone clearly do not explain the British case. British public support for the war has not shown any significant drop in direct response to casualty spikes. Moreover, British support remains now where it was in 2006 in spite of the fact that over 85 percent of Britain's 239 casualties have occurred since then. There is insufficient data to reject logarithmic casualties as an explanation for the British case, but Mueller would struggle to explain the stabilization of support, and the apparent rally in early 2009.

By contrast, elite discord, the use by political leaders of multiple rationales and diminishing prospects for success on the ground have all had important effects. Well-informed, nonpartisan figures within the British elite with strong backgrounds in military and foreign affairs, such as Max Hastings and Rory Stewart, have very effectively cast doubt over the course and likelihood of success of the mission, especially when leaked comments from the military and Foreign Office suggest many serving officers share their misgivings.

Lack of multilateral burden sharing has not been a major factor. The best evidence—the reaction to President Sarkozy's decision to increase the French presence in the south—suggests multilateral support has little influence on the trajectory of public support in the UK.

It is hard to tell whether the shift to a counterinsurgency/nation-building mission has had a significant impact—opinion polls on Afghanistan simply do not exist for the relevant time period.

Again, however, the progress of the war on the ground emerges as a strong factor. British public support for the war appears to be the most sensitive to incoming news suggesting that the Allied cause is heading for defeat. A senior officer or diplomat quoted as saying that the war effort cannot succeed has a far more significant effect on public opinion than even substantial losses of life. Moreover, the fact that support for the war in Britain has held up reasonably well around the 35-40 percent mark since 2006 suggests that the solid hawks that Feaver and Gelpi identified in the United States have an approximately equally sized counterpart in Britain.

Finally, shifting rationales have most likely been a misjudgment of British policymakers in trying to rally support for the war. British leaders cycled through various rationales between 2006 and 2008, and public support fell. Conversely, by 2009, the British leadership made a concerted effort to tighten up its rhetorical strategy on Afghanistan. This bore some fruit for them in terms of stabilizing public support for the war. However, by the end of 2009, they had moved back to the more scattergun rhetorical strategy of 2006—and public support dropped again accordingly.

In short, four factors—increasing casualties, elite discord, shifting and confusing rhetoric from political leaders and the deterioration of the situation on the ground in Afghanistan—have combined to undermine public support for the war in Britain.

FAREWELL TO THE BLUE HELMETS—CANADIAN PUBLIC OPINION ON AFGHANISTAN

Canada is often believed to be a nation defined by its distaste for the perceived belligerence of its southern neighbor. Canada bears such a high degree of cultural resemblance to the United States that engaging in "nice cop" behavior such as contributing foreign aid and engaging in UN-sanctioned peacekeeping operations is said by many to be its main way of differentiating itself from the Americans. This attitude was expressed well by Canadian Foreign Minister Bill Graham MP during the Bosnian conflict:

> We have a moral superiority in dealing with our American colleagues at this time because of the tremendous contribution our troops are making (to the peacekeeping operation).[190]

Prior to the Afghan war, it was assumed by many that this Canadian stereotype meant that the Canadian public would never accept their forces deployed in any kind of warfighting, as opposed to peacekeeping, role. Yet the stereotype of the pacifist-inclined Canadians is a recent creation, and does not entirely reflect the history and attitudes of the Canadian people.

The image of Canada as the world's blue helmeted peacekeeper largely dates back to the age of former Prime Minister Lester Pearson.[191] Prior to the 1950s and 1960s, Canada had not differed noticeably from other Commonwealth countries such as Australia in its willingness to contribute towards decidedly unilateral missions in support of the British Empire. Canadian troops contributed to the British war effort in the wars in the Sudan, the Boer War, World Wars I and II, and the Korean War. Unlike the other reputed pacifist in this analysis, Germany, Canada emerged from World War II with an enhanced national reputation for its vital contribution to the defeat of Hitler. Although the Canadian military had not engaged in a "hot" war since Korea and had participated in numerous UN-sanctioned peacekeeping operations, the leadership of the Canadian forces bristled at the "blue helmet" image of their service, and by 9/11 were keen to be given the chance to prove their warfighting credentials.[192]

Canadian public attitudes for the use of force and casualty tolerance also give lie to the popular image of the pacifist Canadian. Pew Global's 2004 survey on attitudes to the legitimacy of force in international affairs revealed 71 percent of Canadians believed it legitimate to use force to "maintain order in the world" — a higher figure than in confirmed interventionist nations such as the UK or France and almost as high as in the United

States.[193] In the Balkan conflicts, opinion polling prior to 9/11 indicated a greater hypothetical casualty tolerance among Canadians than among most Europeans (for example, a 1999 poll revealed that Canadians had the highest level of support of any country polled except for the ancient Serbian rival, Croatia, for a ground invasion of Kosovo).[194] Opinion polls through 1994-95 consistently demonstrated over 60 percent support for the Canadian mission in Bosnia.[195] Moreover, Canada, with the United States, Britain, and the Netherlands, is one of only four NATO countries that did not impose parliamentary caveats on their troops prior to engagement in Afghanistan.[196]

Thus, even if by 2001 the Canadian public had grown unused to the idea of their military engaged in a warfighting role overseas, the potential support for such a deployment among the Canadian people had been much underestimated. It would be inaccurate to class Canada with the more pacifically inclined European nations such as Germany. The attitudes of the Canadian public in fact more closely resemble those of Australia or Britain.

In terms of anti-Americanism, polling data show that Canada's much vaunted rivalry with its southern neighbor in fact masks a very warm and close relationship. The CBC polls for the multinational project, "What the World thinks of America," revealed the Canadians to be consistently the most pro-American of the participating nations besides Israel. The United States had a net favorability rating in Canada of 81 percent. On balance, 66 percent of Canadians believed the United States to be a force for good in the world, again second only to Israel. The number of Canadians agreeing that "America has reaped the thorns sown by its rulers in the world" was 56 percent, second lowest after the UK and Israel; 72 percent of Canadians responded that the United States is a beacon of hope and opportunity, again second only to Israel.[197] Canada, in short, is probably the most pro-American country in this sample besides the United States itself.

When Jean Chretien's Liberal Government initially deployed troops to Afghanistan in the aftermath of 9/11, therefore, one could reasonably predict that Canadian support for the mission would be reasonably robust. However, the Canadian forces' long hiatus from aggressive warfighting might have left some doubts as to how the Canadian public would respond if Canada became involved in heavy combat. Seven years after the initial deployment, the Canadian forces have won a new reputation for counterinsurgency warfare and dispelled their image as a purely peacekeeping military. However, the war has caused heavy Canadian casualties, heated controversy at home and support, which had been as high as 70 percent in 2006[198], has fallen to 42 percent according to the latest polls,[199] and has been lower still at times.

I will now outline an explanation for this trend.

Casualties.

Logarithmic Casualties. The Canadian polling data on Afghanistan are very extensive. As Canada was not a participant in Iraq, the Iraq war did not overshadow Afghanistan in the news media or the polls as happened in the UK, Australia, and the United States. At the same time, because Canada was involved in the combat in Afghanistan and frequently has taken casualties, the war did not simply fall out of the public eye for extended periods as happened in France and Germany. This allows us to track the decline of public support very closely.

The picture of a direct, logarithmic response to casualties would be misleading. As can be seen from Figures 12 and 13, the trajectory of Canadian public opinion does not conform to the picture of one short sharp drop followed by a more sedate decline thereafter. Rather there is a short sharp decline as the insurgency heats up in 2006, followed by something of a switchback before settling into a steady pattern of approximately 60 percent opposition and 40 percent support from late 2007 onwards.

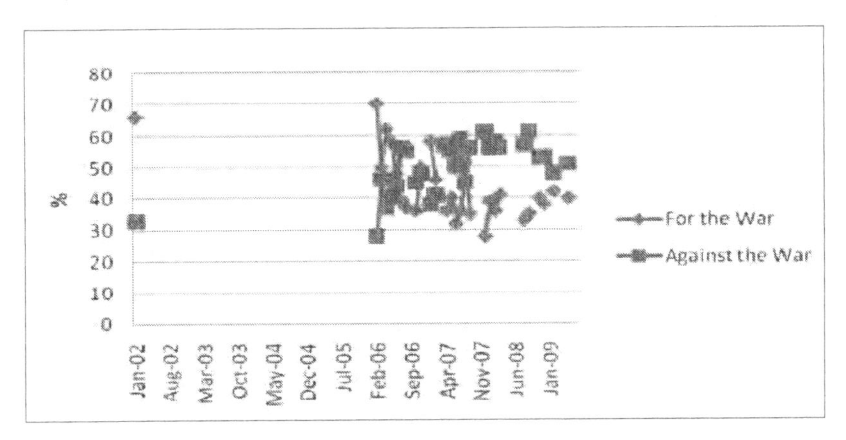

Figure 12. Canadian Public Opinion and the War in Afghanistan, 2002-09.

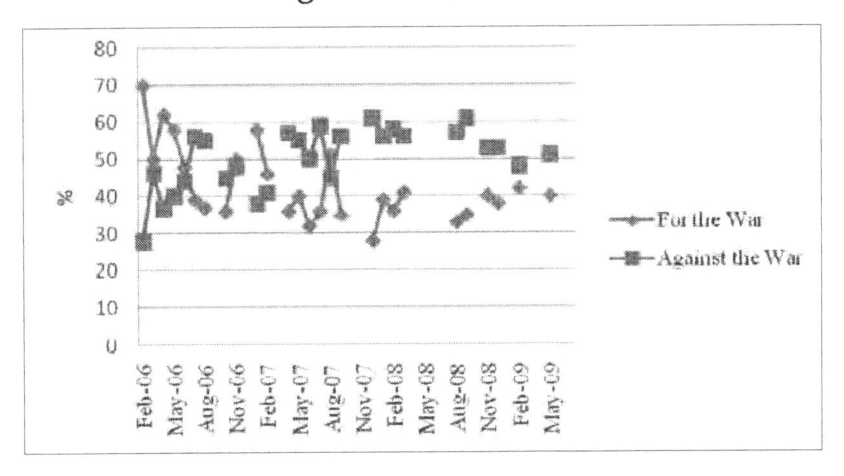

Figure 13. Canadian Public Opinion and the War in Afghanistan, 2006-09.

Marginal Casualties. Again, as with the American and British cases, it has been possible to plot the evolution of public support against casualties over time (see Figure 14). As in the British case, public opinion does not simply respond automatically to the latest casualty figures. For a start, there are the numerous mini-rallies which can be seen in Canadian public opinion. Analysts who believe public opinion is wholly determined by casualties never expect to see public support rally.

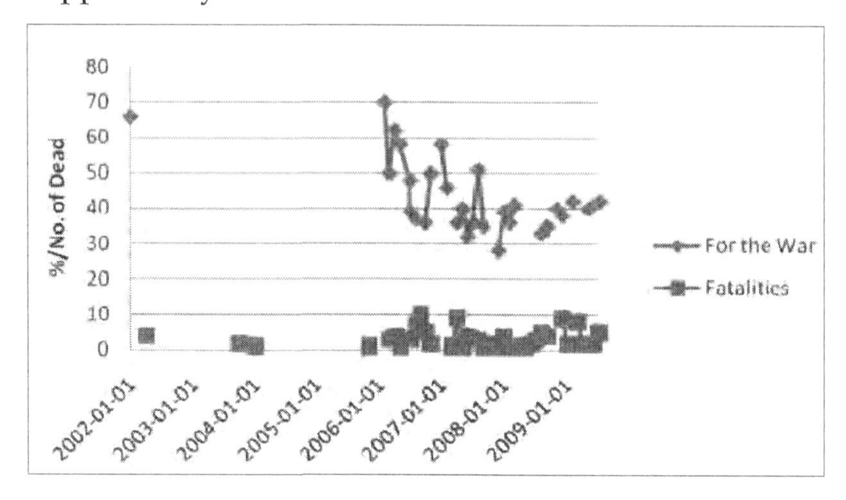

Figure 14. Canadian Support for the War and Fatalities, 2006-09.

Moreover, the spring and early summer of 2006 is when Canadian public opinion first began to turn against the war, with sharp drops in public support. Yet the heaviest casualties do not come until September of that year, by which time the sharpest fall in support had already occurred. Finally, it is hard to see why, as in the British case, a solid core of approximately 30-40 percent of the population has stuck with the operation loyally since the beginning. None of the casualties incurred since late 2007 have had much of an additonal effect on the level of support in Canada.

Clearly, factors other than casualties must be examined to account for the trajectory of support for the war, as in the other cases we have so far reviewed.

Casualties Plus Politics.

Elite Consensus. Canada's initial deployment enjoyed bipartisan support from both the opposition Conservatives and the governing Liberal Party. However, the war has proved unpopular with the smaller Canadian parties such as the leftist National Democrats and the separatist Bloc Quebecois. Moreover, when in opposition, the Liberals began to develop grave misgivings about the mission and, in fact, generated an internal split on the issue. The "Ignatieff" wing of the Liberal Party, led by Liberal MP and public champion of "humanitarian intervention" Michael Ignatieff, supported the Harper Government's extension of the mission in 2007, while other figures such as former leader Stephane Dion voted against the deployment. It is estimated that only the defection of Ignatieff and his supporters in the Liberal Party saved Prime Minister Harper from defeat in the 2006 vote to extend the Canadian mission until 2009.[200] The House of Commons voted again in 2008 to further extend the mission until 2011. The second vote was more decisive and passed with a higher majority. The Harper Government won Liberal support by pledging that 2011 would definitively mark the end of the combat phase of the deployment, and that the interim period from 2009 would see Canadian forces begin to shift to reconstruction and training more than warfighting.[201] Consensus has since been reestablished both within the Liberal Party and between Liberals and Conservatives in support of this position. However, Ignatieff has occasionally sought to placate the anti-war wing of his party by implicitly suggesting Harper wishes to renege on the deal and seeking a public pledge that Canadian troops will indeed go by December 2011.[202]

The Canadian media, by contrast, have seen nothing to resemble the concerted elite anti-war movement seen in Britain. Public intellectuals and academics have been split over the mission.[203] Popular writing on the Afghanistan war, by contrast, has emphasized the more American or British style gung ho heroics of which the Canadian public has been starved since Korea.[204] Media attention of this sort is more likely to bolster than undermine support for Canadian participation.

Can the limited amount of elite dissensus, which pitted the Conservatives and pro-war Liberals against the anti-war Liberals, NDP, and Bloc Quebecois, account for at least part of the fall in support for the war in Canada? The evidence suggests not. For in fact, the Canadian Liberals began to turn against the war only after, and not before, the main drop in public opinion.[205]

Thus elite discord is simply not a key driver of the fall in support for the war in Canada.

Multilateralism. Canada is unquestionably one of the over-contributors to the mission. Moreover, some initial support for the importance of multilateral burden sharing may be found in the Canadian case. Canadian polls consistently indicated a belief that the Canadian forces are shouldering too much of the burden in Afghanistan. Angus Reid polls throughout 2007 showed solid majorities of the Canadian public (64-58 percent) holding this view.[206] This may partly explain the Canadian Senate Defense Committee's 2007 recommendation that Canada should withdraw if further support from other NATO countries was not forthcoming.[207]

It would have been interesting if pollsters had cross-tabulated support for the war with belief that Canada has borne an unfair share of the burden. This could have provided much more compelling evidence that a lack of multilateral support is a key factor. Indeed, one may still have cause to doubt that it is. For when President Sarkozy effectively picked up the gauntlet the Canadian Senate had thrown down by deploying additional French troops to Afghanistan, Canadian support for the war continued to fall unabated.[208]

Thus it is difficult to conclude definitively that a lack of burden sharing has been a significant factor in the drop in support in Canada. Unquestionably, Canadian voters believe that they have borne a disproportionate share of the burden, but too many other factors have also been present to allow one to prove that this itself has had a large independent effect on support for the war as a whole.

Principal Policy Objective. Many analysts who held to the pre-Afghanistan view of Canadian public opinion would question the applicability of the principal policy objective model to Canada. It might have been claimed that foreign policy restraint missions are a sign of un-Canadian belligerence and would not command the popularity north of the border that they would in the United States. As this monograph takes a skeptical tone towards the traditional image of the Canadian public supporting only blue-helmeted peace missions, we will still consider this factor to be potentially important.

Nonetheless, looking at the graph of support through time reveals Canadian public support to have held up well long after the end of the initial "restraint" phase of 2001. Strong majority support for the operation in Canada was evident as late as spring of 2006, long after the mission had come to be defined by counterinsurgency and internal political change.

Again, it seems that the change in principal policy objective is not the key driver of the fall in support.

Prospects of Success. Close analysis of the timeline of Canadian support and the events of the war lends a great deal of credence to the importance of the prospects for success.

Canadian public opinion began to turn decisively against the war in the spring and summer of 2006.[209] In February, polls indicated support for the war running at 70 percent.[210] This began to drop sharply over the spring and summer, although polls remained volatile, with different polls in June giving a majority against and a plurality in favor of the war.[211] However, after January 2007, no poll has shown a majority in favor and the polls in 2008 have shown opinion hardening against the war.[212] The decisive turning points appear to be spring-summer 2006 and winter 2007.[213]

The spring-summer 2006 turning points are consistent with both an account that hinges solely on casualties and with one in which prospects for success are key. Spring-summer 2006 saw Canadian forces take the heaviest casualties of all NATO forces in fighting around Kandahar.[214] This same fighting also revealed that the Taliban had recovered decisively from 2002 and that the Afghanistan War had become an intense counterinsurgency campaign. However, Canadian public opinion still held up to some degree even after the summer of 2006. Indeed, as stated above, some polls still showed majority support as late as January 2007.[215] However, the following month, the Canadian Senate Committee on Defense and National Security published a report in which they concluded that "the Taliban have time and geography on their side" and recommended that Canada should consider withdrawal if greater support from other NATO countries was not forthcoming.[216] Then in May 2007, the Afghan Parliament's Upper House passed a resolution urging that negotiations be started immediately with any Taliban who were willing to join the Government. To be sure, an additional 22 Canadian troops were killed in the first half of 2007.[217] However, there is a sharp drop in support between January and February 2007 (17 percent)[218] immediately following the release of the Senate Report, but in neither month did the Canadian Forces suffer any casualties.

Moreover, the pattern identified by Feaver and Gelpi, can also explain the relative stability of Canadian opinion since late 2007.

By December 2007, the Canadian equivalents of the defeat and casualty phobes had turned against the mission, leaving only the solid hawks. Almost 40 percent of Canada's total casualties have been incurred since then.[219] This includes some brutal casualty shocks in December 2008 and March 2009. But there have been no further lasting or noticeable drops in Canadian support since December 2007, a fact which, as in the British case, strongly suggests the existence of a group of solid hawks.

Again, then, as in the British and Canadian cases, the evidence in favor of a strong effect of prospects for success on the trajectory of support is good. Indisputably, though, other factors are also at play in the Canadian case.

Afghanistan-Specific Theories.

Confused Rationales. In the Canadian case, it is easy to see why Parliament's Manley Commission and observers such as Professor Stein have concluded that political leaders have failed to outline the strategic aim of the war in clear terms. Prior to the renewed Canadian deployment to Kandahar in 2005, Foreign Secretary Bill Graham and Chief of the Defense Staff General Rick Hillier engaged on a speaking tour across Canada designed to rally public support, billed in the media as a "pre-body bag" tour. However, Graham and Hillier gave justifications for the Canadian involvement that contradicted one another and left the public confused as to the real reasons for the deployment. Graham stated:

> Our role in Afghanistan is quintessentially Canadian: we are helping to rebuild a troubled country and we are giving hope for the future to a long suffering people. This is a clear expression of our Canadian values at work.[220]

However, at the same time as Graham was posing as the great humanitarian, General Hillier took on a more warlike posture:

> Being a soldier means that you go out and bayonet somebody. We are not the public service of Canada. We are not just another Department. We are the Canadian forces and our job is to kill people.[221]

According to Stein, this represented a difference in objectives between the Liberal Government, which was unenthusiastic about the war and believed it was heading a reconstruction mission, and the Canadian military leadership, which wanted to prove themselves in a combat environment after years of resenting the common perception that they were merely a European-style peacekeeping force. Liberal Prime Minister Paul Martin was later to say:

> I had no sense that it was war. I surely didn't think that it was war. It was not presented to me as a counterinsurgency operation. Our purpose was reconstruction.[222]

The confused nature of the reasons for war continued under the Conservative Government of Stephen Harper. Harper's first Defense Secretary, General Gordon O'Connor, added a new rationale for the war when he suggested that the war was about "retribution" for the 9/11 attacks.[223] Harper also curtailed the amount of time given to debate the Afghanistan issue in Parliament, justified the extension of the Canadian deployment only by saying that Canada would not "cut and run" from Afghanistan, and announced that he would extend the mission regardless of the will of Parliament.[224]

Thus at least four separate freestanding justifications for the war can be found in the rhetoric of Canadian politicians in rallying support for the war—a purely altruistic "pro-bono" humanitarian case, a counterterrorist case, a retribution case, and a reputational case that Canada could not leave its allies to carry the burden alone. In light of this, it is not surprising that many Canadians might have wondered what the real purpose of the war actually was.

Moreover, as an inspection of the timeline of support makes clear, the confused rationales were present in the rhetoric of Canadian leaders from 2005 onwards, but public support for the war was still strong in early 2006 and did not fall sharply until the summer. If there is a causal relationship between confused and shifting rationales and a fall in public support for the war, it can only go from the elite's rhetoric to public support, rather than the other way around.

In contrast to the British case, over 2009, Harper has not attempted to reverse the tide of public opposition by tightening up his public rhetoric on the war. Rather, now that his Government has committed to ceasing combat operations in 2011, Harper has openly voiced skepticism about the Afghanistan mission more characteristic of an opponent of the war—a skepticism born of his experience directing the Canadian war effort and the difficulties this has involved. For example, speaking on Fareed Zakaria's GPS, Harper stated that:

> There are enormous risks there for us and there are enormous challenges and I'm not saying we cannot improve things, but our experience has taught us that if we think we can govern Afghanistan for the Afghans and be responsible for their security day-by-day then we are mistaken...The issue Canadians ask is whether we are being successful. We are not going to win this war just by staying. We are not going to, in fact my own judgment is we are not going to defeat the insurgency, in fact my reading of Afghan history is that they've had an insurgency forever. . . . If the source of authority is perceived as being foreign, it will always have some degree of opposition.[225]

In contrast to the UK, then, we cannot tell whether a shift away from multiple rationales would have stemmed the trend of public support for the war in Canada. Had Harper attempted to tighten up Canadian rhetoric and win back support for the war in a similar fashion to Brown and Milliband, it would have been interesting to see if Canadian support would have revived somewhat, as British support has in 2009.

However, the lack of one clear overriding rationale is most likely a very important factor in explaining the fall in support in Canada. Opinion polls have sought to ascertain Canadians' opinions on Harper's explanations for the war as well as for the war itself. Tellingly, the numbers who believe his explanation to be poor and the numbers favoring immediate withdrawal are very close—in one poll 59 percent and 56 percent, respectively. In that same September 2007 poll, long after Canadian troops had commenced heavy combat with the Taliban, Canadian respondents were almost evenly split between those who believed Afghanistan to be a war mission and those who believed it to be a peace mission—44 percent believed it to be a peace mission, 36 percent to be a war mission, with 19 percent unsure.[226] This latter fact is especially strong evidence that the Harper Government had failed to explain the mission thoroughly.

Conclusion.

The Canadian case is a rich source of information on the causes of the decline in support for the war. Again, casualties alone are not the key factor. Likewise, elite discord is more a symptom than a cause of the breakdown of public support for the war.

The diminishing prospects for success are key, when one examines closely the trend in support for war over time. At the same time, confusing and shifting rationales by Canadian policymakers have also had a major effect, as in Britain. Canadian polling evidence suggests this strongly. Even stronger evidence could have been available if the Harper Government had taken the Manley Report's recommendations on board and tightened its rhetoric on the war, and this had led to a stabilization of support as in Britain in 2009. However, as Harper himself has largely moved to a skeptical position on the war, this natural experiment did not take place.

SARKOZY'S WAR—FRANCE TAKES TO THE FRONTLINE

In spite of the popular American jibe about "cheese-eating surrender monkeys," the preexisting attitudes of the French public and political elite to international intervention and military casualties were by all expert accounts very robust. As the Pew Global poll cited above revealed, the French public's attitudes to the legitimacy of the use of force in international affairs are indistinguishable from the British and far closer to the Americans than to the Germans. The French tied with the British at 67 percent in approving the proposition that it is legitimate to use force to maintain order overseas.[227] France participated in multilateral interventions in Somalia, the first Gulf War and Bosnia. The French Army has in addition frequently intervened in military disputes in former French colonies—from Operation TURQUOISE in support of the Rwandan Hutus in the 1990s to the armed intervention in the Ivory Coast in 2004.[228] Professor Theo Farrell of King's College London, having carried out focus group work with the French officer corps, termed the French "a true war-fighting military."[229] This need not necessarily be indicative of robust civilian attitudes to the use of force, but the two most often go hand in hand. Natalie La Balme, interviewing French policymakers, claimed that a typical response to the fear of casualties in overseas intervention was: "If zero deaths is the objective, the mission is bound to fail."[230] La Balme's work also revealed high levels of support in France for a variety of theoretical missions—70-88 percent in favor of missions to destroy an unspecified "terrorist training camp" between 1988 and 1998, and 73-77 percent in favor of "risking one's life to defend the values of our society such as freedom and human rights."[231] Indeed, this tracks rather well with French public opinion on real interventions in the 1990s—50-70 percent of French respondents supported the war in Kosovo through the spring of 1999, and strong majorities also supported French participation in the first Gulf War and in Operation RESTORE HOPE in Somalia.[232] In short, the French can support tough military action and French casualties, but they are less likely to do so if they feel the engagement is designed to serve the interests of nations other than France, especially if one of these nations is the United States.

For although popular American stereotypes of French military weakness are wide of the mark, there are hard data to support the accusation of widespread French anti-Americanism. As one of the participating countries in the "What the World thinks of America" survey, France gave the United States a new favorability rating of 41 percent, meaning that on balance more French respondents had an unfavorable than favorable view of America. This figure is substantially lower than the Canadian, British, and Australian totals, and is, in fact, lower even than the figure in Russia.[233] Only 35 percent of French respondents believed the United States was a force for good in the world—far lower than in the UK, Australia, or Canada and almost as low as in Indonesia.[234] Most startlingly, 76 percent of French respondents agreed that "America is reaping the thorns planted by its rulers in the world" —the highest response of the this sample.[235] Pew Global's survey of anti-Americanism traced French attitudes over time and reached similar conclusions—although in 2000 over 60 percent of French respondents had a favorable attitude to the United States, by 2008 this had fallen to 42 percent, having been even lower at the height of the Iraq War.[236] Moreover, the percentage of respondents in France who believed the war on terror to be sincerely aimed at eliminating terrorism was 16 percent lower than in the UK at 35 percent.[237] French voters were even 10 percent less likely to consider U.S. pop culture a "good" thing than their British counterparts, and were 21 percent more likely to believe the spread of U.S. ideas and customs to be "bad." Finally 90 percent of French voters believed it would be a "good" thing if the EU were as powerful as the United States, compared with an even split in the UK.[238]In other polls, although 63 percent of French respondents held al Qaeda responsible for 9/11, 23 percent stated that they did not know.[239]

When President Jacques Chirac ordered the deployment of French troops to Afghanistan in 2001, he therefore had to contend with two preexisting forces which could push French support for the war in opposite directions—an acceptance of the legitimacy of overseas intervention and the inevitability of casualties on the one hand versus a deep-seated distrust of American motives on the other. Consequently, unlike the United States, Great Britain, Canada, and Australia, the French Army has not maintained a continuous presence in southern Afghanistan. When the insurgency resumed the French contingent in Afghanistan was based in the relatively safer Kabul area[240] and had suffered few casualties since Chirac first deployed

French forces in support of Operation ENDURING FREEDOM in 2001. French forces, moreover, do operate under parliamentary caveats like the Germans, although NATO operational secrecy prevents us from knowing what those caveats are.[241] However, unlike its European partner, Germany, France has responded to calls from its allies by placing more of its military forces in the firing line in the Pashtun lands since 2008.[242] This policy reversal was very much the personal decision of President Sarkozy, following his election as President in 2007. This move forms part of Sarkozy's plan to repair France's relations with the United States and reintegrate French forces into the Western alliance, after the deterioration in Franco-American relations that characterized the latter part of his predecessor Jacques Chirac's tenure in office.[243] However, soon after Sarkozy's announcement, the French Army suffered a very politically damaging setback when 10 paratroops were killed in an ambush just outside Kabul.[244] The Taliban followed up with a further blow, when macabre photographs of Taliban fighters wearing the uniforms of the dead French troops were released and published in the popular French magazine, *Paris Match*.[245] The incident led to loud calls for withdrawal by various sections of the French political elite and necessitated Sarkozy's taking the constitutionally unusual step of putting the French military deployment to a vote in Parliament.[246]

In total, France has lost 36 dead over the course of Operation ENDURING FREEDOM. Half of those casualties have come about since Sarkozy announced the redeployment in 2008, with the Kabul incident representing the largest single loss of life in 1 day during the course of the operation.[247] This casualty toll is from a force of over 3,300, making the French casualty rate more or less comparable with Germany's and significantly lower than that of the United States, Canada, or the UK.[248]

French public opinion has followed a very similar arc to the other countries studied here. From 60-70 percent support in late 2001 and early 2002, the Afghan war in France now commands just over 30 percent approval, according to the latest polls.[249] As with all the other countries under study, the Afghan war fell off the political radar in France for many years after the apparent success of the initial invasion in 2001. In fact, the French "polling gap" is even larger than the American or British equivalents. After 2002, French pollsters only began asking about Afghanistan again after Sarkozy's election (but before the redeployment was announced) in 2007.[250] The magnitude of the fall in support in France is somewhat less than in the UK or the United States, but from a slightly lower base. Support for the war in France now stands at almost exactly the same level as in Britain.[251]

The French narrative is therefore somewhat similar to the German—a much greater fall in support than one would predict based solely on French casualties and a comparison with the American, Canadian, and British cases. France, like Germany, appears to have a glass jaw with regard to the Afghan operation. The reasons for this, however, may well be subtly different from those for the German case.

Casualties.

Logarithmic Casualty Sensitivity Models. As discussed above, the data in the French case are very limited, but we can draw some limited inferences by looking at the trend in support over time (See Figure 15).

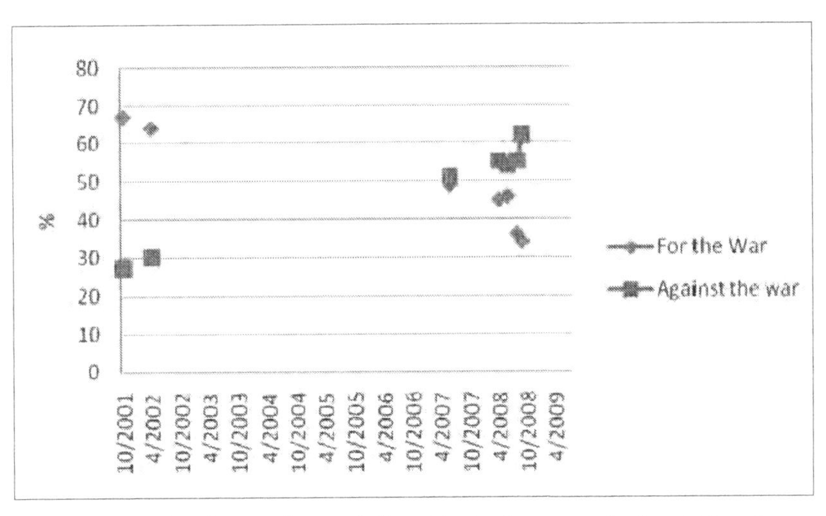

Figure 15. French Public Opinion and the War in Afghanistan, 2001-09.

The picture here does not resemble to any great degree a logarithmic model. Instead of a short sharp drop at the beginning, it appears that support in France held up reasonably well until Sarkozy's decision to increase the troop deployment in 2007. Support then suffered two sharp drops in the latter part of 2007 and then again in the latter part of 2008. It is difficult to be very precise with such limited information, but it seems clear that logarithmic casualty sensitivity cannot tell the whole story.

Marginal Casualties. As we can see from Figure 16 and even more clearly from Figure 17, sharp falls in French support do not, as Gartner and Segura would claim, follow directly from spikes in French casualties. Indeed, the worst spike of all—the summer 2008 ambush—followed rather than preceded a major fall in French approval of the war. Although there is not much data to go on, it seems that casualties alone are no more effective in explaining the French case than any other we have so far studied.

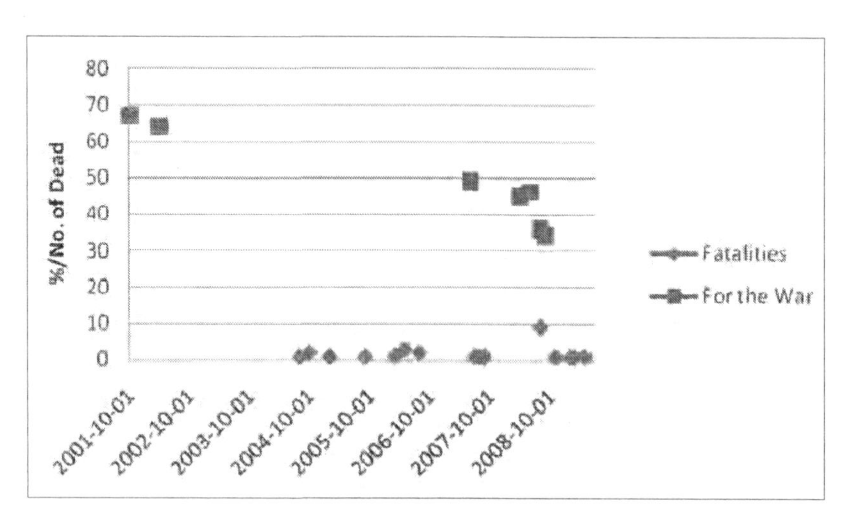

Figure 16. French Support for the War and Fatalities, 2001-09.

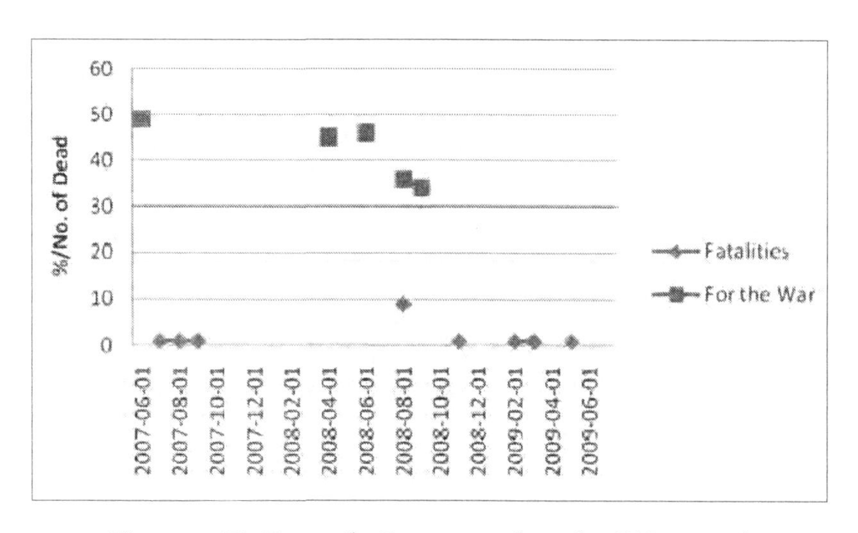

Figure 17. French Support for the War and Fatalities, 2007-09.

Casualties Plus Politics.

Elite Consensus. The decisions to deploy and then to reinforce French troops were taken by different Presidents of the same party— Chirac and Sarkozy of the center right *Rassemblement pour la Republique*, which later merged with other smaller conservative parties to form the modern *Union pour un Mouvement Populaire*.[252] The original decision to deploy troops in 2001 was supported by the other main French party, the center left *Parti Socialiste*, which, at the time of 9/11, formed a majority in parliament while Chirac sat in the Elysee.[253]

However, the reinforcement of the original French mission to Afghanistan and its redeployment to help the United States in the more violent eastern sections of the Pashtun areas broke the French bipartisan consensus. The *Parti Socialiste* condemned the move, and the fact that the announcement was made by President Sarkozy on a visit to London and without a vote in Parliament, although there is nothing in the French constitution which obliges him to hold such a vote.[254] Moreover, as we shall see, even some members of Sarkozy's own party, the UMP, especially the more anti-American Gaullist wing, which had supported Chirac's former foreign minister Dominique de Villepin for the Presidency, also opposed the decision.

As can be seen from the timeline of French support for the war, Sarkozy's decision was followed very quickly by sharp falls in support for the war and the fracturing of the bipartisan consensus. Thus elite discord is clearly a factor in France. Especially important was the ability of the numerous French parliamentary opponents of the war to capitalize on the mistakes made by Sarkozy and his allies in justifying the move to the French people, and to question the prospects for success of the French mission.

Multilateralism. The French case offers a unique twist on the significance of multilateral burden sharing—for in fact the arguments of the French opponents of the war suggested implicitly that helping one's allies is not a sufficient reason to enter a military conflict. Indeed, for many of the more nationalist-inclined French opponents of the war such as Jean-Marie Le Pen or the more hardline Gaullists, any kind of burden sharing by France, even if disproportionately less than other countries, would be unacceptable. Moreover, research on the preexisting attitudes of the French public suggests that this may have found some resonance.

As Natalie La Balme reports, French opinion polls of the 1980s and 1990s recorded that less than half the number of French respondents who were willing to risk their lives to defend France, French values, or French overseas territories, were also willing to do so to defend the territory of French allies.[255]

Moreover, French support, as we have seen, fell very quickly after France moved to pick up a larger share of the burden in the allied operation. In short, multilateral burden sharing is a factor in France, with the modification that many elements of French opinion were opposed to moves to bear any significant share of the burden, let alone a disproportionate one relative to other countries.

Principal Policy Objective. Unlike with multilateralism, it is hard to detect an influence of the change in principal policy objective on the French case. We know that French support had fallen somewhat between the time of the initial invasion in 2002 and the redeployment by Sarkozy in 2007, by which time the principal policy objective had undoubtedly changed, but it is difficult to tell when the fall in support between 2002 and 2007 occurred and whether it was gradual or sudden. Moreover, the sharpest reductions in support occurred shortly after the redeployment decision in 2007, by which time it had been clear that the principal policy objective had been different for some time.

Prospects for Success. This same lack of data makes it difficult to trace the responsiveness of public opinion to the prospects of success. In the American and Canadian cases, we saw how public support dropped in response to the increasing evidence of the resurgence of the Taliban over the summer of 2006. However, because French polls do not resume until 2007, we cannot see whether there was a similar effect in France. At least, however, we cannot reject the prospects for success explanation for France on these grounds either because we know that by 2007 support had dropped from its initial highs.

Stronger evidence for an effect comes from looking at the two other major drops in support, which we can pinpoint in time more effectively. The two summer Taliban offensives of 2007 and 2008 coincide very approximately with those two drops. It was also becoming clear to the worldwide news media at that time that control of the war was slipping away from the Western allies, and the French news media was no exception. *Le Monde*'s headline of August 2007 spoke of "Mr. Bush and Mr. Karzai faced with failure in Afghanistan."[256] Paris-based think-tank IRIS in the same month in 2008 spoke of "The Western Community in Failure in Afghanistan":

> What must be done? No solution other than negotiation with the Taliban is possible, and that is what President Karzai has begun to do anyway, seeing in it his only hope of political survival. The British too are well aware that the hope of a military victory is in the nature of an illusion.[257]

As the latter sentence suggests, the French news media have also given wide exposure to doubters about the Afghanistan war in other countries—the reservations of British Brigadier Carleton-Smith and Ambassador Cowper-Coles (whose remarks were initially leaked to the press by sources in the French embassy) were widely reported in the French press:

> A British General Predicts Failure in Afghanistan . . . Jean-Francois Fitou, number two at the French Embassy in Kabul, cites the British Ambassador Sir Sherard Cowper Coles as claiming "the current strategy of the Americans is doomed to failure. . . . His French counterpart [Fitou] wrote "the current situation is bad, security and corruption are getting worse and the Afghan Government has lost all credibility."[258]

In spite of the paucity of data in the French case, then, it is clear that the diminishing prospects for success of the operation have played an important role. Indeed, the concern that the Afghan operation risks failure is one of the clearest reasons given by the *Parti Socialiste* for their opposition to Sarkozy's redeployment. As party spokesperson Ariane Gil put it:

> We cannot and we must not lose this war, the President tells us. "Who can believe that adding war on top of more war will make the war stop, when we have learned no lessons from the current failure?" replied the Mayor of Nantes. The danger which France faces is more or less that of sinking into a morass. The Socialists refuse to sink into a war without a goal and without an end.[259]

This has also characterized the rhetoric of Socialist MPs in opposition to the war in Parliament, as will be shown below.

In short, the combination of partisan splits over the war and the diminishing prospects for success have combined to exert a powerful downward effect on French support for the war.

Afghanistan-Specific Theories.

Confused Rationale. French political rhetoric, beginning with Chirac in 2001, initially closely resembled that of other participating countries. A variety of different themes emerge, including the need to defend international security against Islamist terrorism, a humanitarian desire to improve the lives of the Afghan people, the war on drugs, and a desire to be a good ally and to be seen to be contributing one's fair share. Again, the important linkages between the humanitarian and security rationales spring up frequently—French leaders have stressed that only a stable, democratic, and prosperous Afghanistan can be guaranteed not to become once again a haven for international terrorism.

Shortly after the beginning of military action in Afghanistan, President Chirac and Prime Minister Tony Blair issued a joint statement designed to prepare their publics for combat and potential losses in Afghanistan:

> The United Kingdom and France reiterate that they stand shoulder to shoulder with the United States and the American people in the fight against terrorism. This is a cause we share with all democratic countries.
>
> Military action is designed to root out the al Qaeda network and the Taliban regime which has protected it. Thereafter we and our partners in the European Union will not turn our backs on Afghanistan. We have pledged to contribute generously to its reconstruction. In this respect, the behavior of the new Afghan leaders will constitute a deciding factor. We recognize that over twenty years of war have shattered Afghan society, brought immense human suffering and left the country without functioning institutions. We will work together

to help return Afghanistan to normality in accordance with the wishes of the Afghan people. Among our key aims will be to create conditions which facilitate the return of refugees to Afghanistan and bring about a resumption of economic activity. . . .

We will work together with the UN and the Afghan parties towards an Afghanistan free of conflict, at peace with its neighbors, with a stable government that works for economic development and respects human rights, especially those of women, and has no place for terrorists, drug smuggling or extremism.[260]

Over the years, Chirac's public statements on Afghanistan differ little from those of his British, Canadian, or German counterparts. As host of the International Conference on Drug Routes, in Paris in 2003, Chirac placed as great an emphasis on combating the drug trade as British policymakers such as John Reid:

Today we are concerned and mobilized by Afghanistan, because what is happening there is a threat to its own stability, that of its neighbors and to international security.

Just over a year ago, Afghanistan freed itself from the Taliban, who had terrorized their own great people and provided a support base for terrorist networks throughout the world. Through a terrible chain of circumstances, Afghanistan has become one of the world's leading opium producers in the space of a few years. It earned this sad honor during a time of conflict and an absence of government, when faced with the necessities of survival and in response to a strong external demand for opium and heroin.

Despite the ban upheld by the Afghan government in January 2002, the United Nations reports that opium now accounts for one fifth of Afghanistan's national income. The response is through law enforcement. Afghanistan, which must rebuild everything, must also

> build a security system. It is now doing so with the assistance of the international community. But we also know that we have to offer an alternative to the three million Afghans who now earn their living by producing drugs, and that development strategies will not produce results until several years from now. We must take energetic measures to attack the whole market-the ever-stronger external demand as well as the supply.[261]

Like his German counterparts, Chirac also stressed the importance of France making a fair contribution alongside its allies: "We know that the international effort will last for years to come, and France will fully play its part."[262] However, as a traditional Gaullist, Chirac could not pledge support to the Allied war effort without making certain gestures towards French and European independence from the United States. For example, he resisted expanding NATO's role in the Afghan operation between 2001 and 2005 and instead made a serious attempt to have control over the reconstruction section of the mission handed over to the newly created Eurocorps, principally staffed and controlled by the French and Germans.[263]

This stands in marked contrast to the approach favored by his successor Sarkozy. Often dubbed "Sarko the American" for his pro-U.S. views,[264] Sarkozy's drive for a more active French role in Afghanistan is part of a number of moves he has made in an attempt to integrate France more closely with its Western allies, including rejoining NATO's unified command.[265] However, his election in 2007 should not be seen as marking a groundswell of pro-American feeling in France, still less a strong desire to beef up the French commitment to Afghanistan. The 2007 election was fought principally on domestic issues[266] and indeed Sarkozy even hinted at one stage in the campaign that he was considering withdrawing French troops from the Afghan campaign altogether.[267] As the decision to deepen France's involvement in Afghanistan was largely Sarkozy's personal choice, but one that was not on his election platform nor even strongly hinted at in advance, France's shift to greater participation in the Afghan war was essentially random. It thus allows us to study the effects of more serious commitment and higher casualties on public opinion in greater depth and draw interesting implications about the possible effects of a similar shift in other European countries.

At the time of Sarkozy's election, French public support for the war had declined from its highs in 2001-2002. France was now split almost 50-50.[268]

The rhetoric of President Sarkozy and other top members of his administration such as Prime Minister Francois Fillon and Foreign Minister Bernard Kouchner (like Joschka Fischer, a former 1960s radical turned humanitarian interventionist) has differed from that of previous French leaders. Sarkozy and his team have tended to make grander statements about Western civilization and a battle between freedom and oppression. In the aftermath of the Kabul ambush, President Sarkozy stated: "My determination remains intact. France is resolved to pursue the fight against terrorism, for democracy and liberty. The cause is just, it is the honor of France and its armies to defend it."[269]

In the debate in the French parliament subsequent to the ambush, Prime Minister Fillon claimed: "If we believe in universal values, we must take the risk of struggling for them." The General-Secretary of Sarkozy's UMP party, Patrick Devedjian, spoke in a similar vein:

> What is happening in Kabul is in reality a fight for the freedom of our society... The Taliban are trying to take back control of the country and if that happens Afghanistan would become terrorism central.[270]

At the same time, more emphasis has been placed on the duty of France to contribute fairly towards a joint Allied effort. Devedjian also stated that:

> There are 45 countries also engaged in Afghanistan. For us to withdraw would be short-sighted.[271]

Foreign Minister Kouchner combined both themes in his speech to Parliament prior to the vote on the deployment:

> You say that we are aligning ourselves with the Americans. On the contrary, we are in the process of defining a common position among the 25 European countries. . . . I remain persuaded that we must not abandon our Afghan friends.[272]

Defense Minister Herve Morin leaned more heavily on the importance of France fulfilling its responsibility to its Allies in the same debate:

> How can we talk of retreat when France is a permanent member of the UN security council and has voted for every UN resolution authorizing the Afghan force since 2001? How can you talk of retreat Noel Mamere (Green Party Deputy) when France is the current President of the European Union and 25 of the 27 member states are engaged in Afghanistan? Our departure would be a dramatic sign of a lack of will of one country while the entire international community is fighting terrorism.[273]

Finally, the UMP's parliamentary leader Jean-Francois Cope:

> You do not have the right to abandon our Afghan friends! Voting for a retreat today would be to capitulate to an ideology which considers the lives of others to be worth nothing, and the lives of women to be worth even less. Voting for the withdrawal of our troops today is to betray our values and our responsibilities without improving our security. On the contrary: remember Churchill: 'if you choose dishonor to avoid war, you will end up with dishonor AND war'. Leaving Afghanistan would be irresponsible. It would be the first domino to fall, risking toppling many others, starting with Pakistan.[274]

However, Sarkozy's and his allies' rhetoric failed to effectively rally French support around the war. On the contrary, the summer of 2008, over which the Kabul ambush set alight the debate in France of which the comment above is a selection, saw French public opinion decisively shift against the Afghan mission. An Ifop Poll in April of 2008 showed majority opposition, but still a very closely run affair—55 percent opposed versus 45 percent in favor.[275] However, by September support had dropped a further 12 percent to 34 percent.[276]

Why were the UMP's attempts to rally support so counterproductive? Obviously the 10 casualties in August and the ensuing Paris Match affair were very damaging; however, one must also cite the shortcomings of the Sarkozy administration's rhetorical strategy.

For a public rationale for the war that leans so heavily on fulfilling one's obligations to Allies, especially the United States and Britain, is a risky strategy for a country such as France with a historically prickly relationship with the "Anglo-Saxons."

Unfortunately, by stressing primarily obligations to Allies as the motivating cause for French engagement, Sarkozy and others may have given the impression that French participation in the war was motivated mostly by a desire to please the Americans.

Hard data on French attitudes to the multilateral use of force and to the United States are not hard to come by. Ifop polls in 2008 reveal that a significantly larger proportion of the French public—47 percent to 38 percent—believe that defending the French homeland should take priority over securing unstable regions of the world.[277]

French anti-Americanism, both a source and a product of anti-American rhetoric from French Presidents as diverse as Charles de Gaulle and Francois Mitterand, can be easily exploited by opponents of the Afghan war. In a country whose public is suspicious of foreign policy initiatives not explicitly designed to serve French interests, suspicious of the United States and of the war on terror, the belief that French soldiers are risking their lives for the benefit of America is a potent rallying cry. Most notoriously, the leader of the Front National, Jean Marie Le Pen, released a statement shortly after the Kabul ambush deploring the French engagement in the following terms:

> These soldiers were doing their duty. But they did not die for France. They died in the interminable war which the United States of America is conducting in that country for its own interests. The deaths of our soldiers underlines cruelly how Nicholas Sarkozy is leading a disastrous policy of alignment with the United States. France has no business being in Afghanistan. Our soldiers do not have to get themselves killed for Uncle Sam.[278]

Le Pen, although on the extreme right of the political spectrum, represents a nontrivial proportion of the French population, having won 11 percent of the vote in the 2007 election.[279] Moreover, his views were echoed, though in less blunt language, by many more mainstream figures on both left and right. In the September 2008 debate, Green Party Deputy Noel Mamere stated:

> We refuse to see our children's blood spilt in a cause which is not theirs.[280]

Even members of Sarkozy's own UMP party, holding more traditionally Gaullist anti-American views, spoke out against the French engagement. For example, Jean-Pierre Grand stated:

> I will vote in support of the French Army but in no case is my vote to be taken as a sign of support for a foreign policy which I find too Atlanticist.[281]

Similarly, Jacques Myard, again of the UMP, spoke of grave misgivings and his belief that French interests were being sacrificed to American ones.

> I do not approve of sending reinforcements to Afghanistan and I am abstaining in consequence. We must get ourselves out of this Afghan quagmire. It is clear that the conduct of this war is controlled, dominated and imposed by the Americans upon whom we exercise no influence whatsoever. We must withdraw from front line combat while maintaining our efforts to train the Afghan Army.[282]

The opposition Socialist Party (PS) has also swung against the war, although in more measured language than the anti-war sections of the French right. The PS's parliamentary leader, Jean-Marc Ayrault, stated:

> We are not voting against the pursuit of the French engagement. We are voting against a political and military strategy which is leading us into an impasse. We are sliding into a war of occupation without time limits or objectives. It is not the vocation of this intervention, nor France's conception, nor in the interests of Afghanistan.[283]

As we have seen in previous statements from the more moderate socialists, their principal objection is more the perceived likelihood of failure for the operation, rather than its association with the United States, although both arguments may be discerned in Ayrault's speech.

Further out to the left, the Communist Party, still a small but significant player in French politics shared some of the anti-American rhetoric of its supposed polar opposite Le Pen:

> We believe it is necessary that the political and social forces which wish to react to this situation (the death of 10 French troops in Afghanistan) express their opposition to the war and to France's foreign policy which is aligned with Washington and integrated completely into NATO.[284]

In sum then, the rhetoric of French opponents of the war, while echoing their counterparts in the United States, UK, Canada, and Germany in raising concerns about strategy and the prospects for success of the war, has contained a strong hint of anti-Americanism unique to the French case. Anti-war politicians of left and right have successfully portrayed the war as driven by Sarkozy's desire to ingratiate himself with the Americans rather than by a clear conception of France's national interest. Unfortunately, by talking very little about why the Afghanistan deployment is in France's own security interests, Sarkozy and his team have given unwitting help to their opponents.

The diminishing prospects for success and French casualties have combined with the breakdown of the bipartisan consensus and the Sarkozy Government's weak and shifting rhetorical justification for the war to produce an over-determined fall in public support. France, like Germany, has a glass jaw. This glass jaw is the inability of her political leaders to explain the Afghan deployment in terms of France's own national security. French support for the war would not have dropped as quickly and as far as it has if it were not for this. French opponents of the war have, and French supporters of the war have not, found a narrative to describe the Afghan war in ways that resonate with a French people suspicious of the United States and warily protective of France's national interest.

STILL STRUGGLING WITH THE GUILT OF THE PAST: GERMANY'S AFGHAN AGONIES

In the years prior to 9/11, it had appeared that Germany was beginning to normalize its attitude to the use of force in international affairs. Following the German constitutional court's decision legitimizing so called "out-of-area" missions, German troops participated in peacekeeping operations in Bosnia and Macedonia and German aircraft participated in their first shooting war since 1945 in Kosovo.[285] German public opinion remained solid throughout the Kosovo conflict, never dropping below 50 percent and sometimes reaching above 60 percent.[286] In this respect, Germans were more enthusiastic about Kosovo than many other Europeans and (at times) more than the Americans, but Kosovo was a particular case for the German public because of its relative proximity to Germany and because the alleged use of genocide by Milosevic evoked a response of "Never again Auschwitz" from sections of the German people.[287]

In terms of their attitudes to the international use of force, Zoltan Juhasz's research emphasized the finding that a majority of Germans in the early 1990s were prepared to use force to defend their homeland.[288] However, this is a very minimal standard for the legitimacy of the use of force, and in the formerly communist East Germany almost 50 percent of the population was not willing to use force to do so. Moreover, Juhasz's polls revealed only a minority in West or East Germany to be prepared to support out of area missions for the Bundeswehr.[289] A decade later, the Pew Global Attitudes Project - 2007 revealed some striking statistics about the relative strengths of pacifist feeling in Europe and North America. Asked whether "the use of military force to maintain order is sometimes justified," a clear majority of Germans—58-41 percent—answered that it was not. This is the only country in this analysis for which this is true. The figures for the United States were 77 percent in favor and 22 percent against, fully 36 percent higher than in Germany. Even the Canadian public, often considered more pacific than their near neighbors, were 71 percent in favor of using military force to maintain order, with only 22 percent against. Britain and France reveal an almost identical attitude—in both countries 66 percent were in favor, with 33 percent of French respondents being against, compared to 28 percent of Britons. This is suggestive of a slightly more pacific attitude in Britain and France than in North America, but still very substantively different (over 25 percent) from Germany.[290]

Thus German attitudes towards the international use of force are strikingly different from all the other countries in this assessment. In terms of anti-Americanism, Germany reveals itself to be somewhere between the English-speaking countries—the UK, Canada and Australia—on the one hand, and France on the other. Although German broadcasters did not participate in the "What the World thinks of America" poll, Pew Global has carried out extensive research into German attitudes towards the United States. German opinion on the United States began the new millennium relatively well, with 78 percent of Germans holding positive views of the United States—only 5 percent lower than in the UK. However, as the decade progressed, German attitudes towards America hardened and fell to 31 percent approval, lower even than France.[291] While 64 percent of Germans blamed al Qaeda for the 9/11 attacks (higher than the corresponding statistic for the UK), fully 23 percent believed it to be the work of the U.S. Government itself.[292]

Thus German public opinion was a difficult and uncomfortable mixture of still strong pacifist feeling and latent anti-Americanism by 2001. Chancellor Gerhard Schroeder would have known he faced a tough task reconciling the German public to close involvement in Afghanistan.

Consequently, the extent and nature of Germany's participation in Afghanistan has been controversial to both supporters and opponents of the war at home and abroad. For the German left, any German military engagement outside of Europe is highly controversial, and a number of German politicians have consistently called for the Bundeswehr's complete withdrawal.[293] Outside of Germany, however, the complaint is rather of a lack of German participation in the war. On a recent visit to Germany, U.S. Secretary of State Hillary Clinton echoed President Barack Obama's appeals for a larger German contribution to the Allied war effort:

> As President Obama has made quite clear, we need our closest allies, like Germany, to help us ensure the success and stability of the Afghan nation at this very important point.[294]

Less diplomatically, many sections of the news media in countries such as the United States, Australia, and the UK have poured scorn on the existing German effort, and all but accused "whining" and "cake-eating" German politicians and troops of cowardice.[295]

The bone of contention between Germany and its NATO allies in Afghanistan is not the raw size of the commitment, but rather the location of the German deployment and the national caveats under which German forces operate. With approximately 4,500 troops in Afghanistan, Germany is numerically the third largest contributor to the Allied war effort.[296] However, German forces have been deployed mostly in the safer, non-Pashtun-speaking northern areas of Afghanistan, away from the center of the insurgency, and German politicians have stoutly resisted calls to move them south. Consequently, the costs of war have been lighter for Germany than for some others. The Germans have lost 34 dead—less than one-fifth the British total, from a force just over half the size of the British deployment. The German death toll is also less than a third of Canada's, even though Canada's force in Afghanistan is smaller than Germany's.

Moreover, the Bundeswehr operates under a series of national caveats which have taken on the character of a joke among other contributing nations—for example, German forces, by the rules of engagement imposed on them by the Bundestag, are not allowed to patrol at night.[297]

Data on the initial levels of support for the war seem to support this story. In the early stages of 2002, the German public supported the war by a margin of 61 percent to 31 percent, 5 percent lower than the total support the war enjoyed in Canada, 12 percent less than the UK and fully 28 percent lower than in the United States.[298] Although no margin of error was provided, this suggests a significant initial gap in support for the war between the Germans and the Anglo-Saxons even in the earliest post 9/11 phase of the Afghan war. Moreover, public opinion in Germany on the war was approaching a 50-50 split even by the summer of 2002, when the war appeared to be all but won and before Germany had suffered any casualties at all.[299]

As with all other participating countries, the apparent success of the Allied effort, and the all-consuming interest in the war in Iraq, meant that the issue dropped off the polling radar in Germany for many years thereafter. The next poll on the subject came in early 2007, and revealed the majority of Germans were opposed to the deployment (57 percent -36 percent).[300] Public opinion fluctuated somewhat in between but has on average flatlined since then. The latest poll, in March 2009, gives a very similar figure of 58 percent opposed and 36 percent in favor.[301]

Casualties.

Unfortunately the sparseness of the polling data in the German case makes it difficult to draw very tight inferences about the causes of the drop in support. Moreover, as German casualties have also been few and far between, it is difficult to draw direct linkages between casualties and that fall in support.

Nonetheless, it is clear that any purely casualties-based explanation has limited weight. A logarithmic casualty sensitivity model cannot explain why support in Germany was significantly lower to begin with than in other NATO countries. Nor can it explain why support began to fall very quickly and before Germany had suffered any casualties at all. Support has shown some responsiveness to recent spikes as in Gartner and Segura's account—a snap poll taken in the aftermath of a suicide bombing that killed three German soldiers in May 2007 (Germany's third heaviest casualties in 1 day since the beginning of the operation)[302] revealed the sharpest drop yet in support, with only 28 percent of Germans supporting the continuation of the mission. However, as we have seen, the drop in support for the war in Germany has been only slightly less steep than in the UK, Canada, or the United States in spite of a death toll that is only a fraction that of the Anglophones. Moreover, unlike in any of the other countries studied, the majority of Germany's (low) casualties came in 2002 and 2003, mostly in nonhostile accidents.[303] However, the trajectory of support for the war seems to have followed the same pattern as in all the rest.[304] (See Figure 18.)

Of course, this is not to say that casualties are not important. The sharp decline in June 2003 demonstrates that they are. Moreover, it is quite plausible that German forces have been kept out of the most dangerous areas of Afghanistan precisely because German leaders have very good reason to believe that the German public is casualty-sensitive to a greater degree than the American or British publics are. Moreover, while it is unlikely that the U.S. opposition, Republicans or the

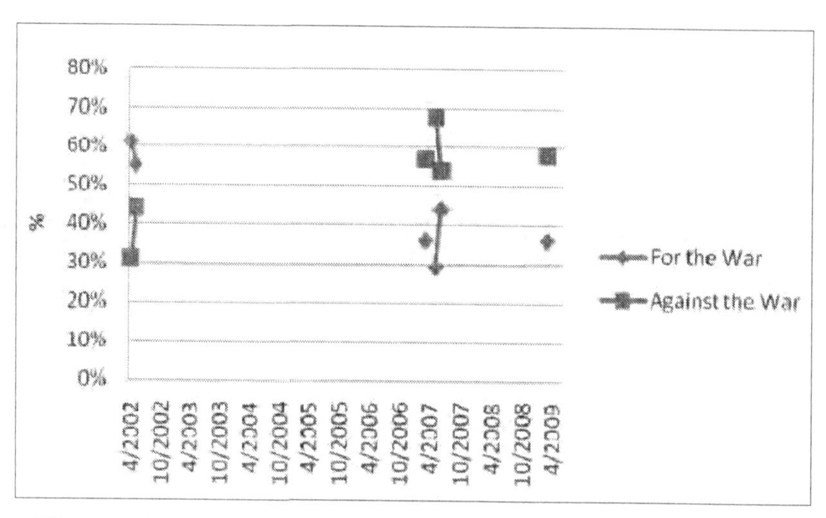

Figure 18. German Public Opinion and the War in Afghanistan, 2002-09.

UK's opposition Conservatives, would seize on additional U.S. or British casualties to advocate withdrawal, it is quite plausible that Chancellor Angela Merkel's main rivals in the center-left SPD could do so in the event of German casualties.[305] Thus the Merkel Government must play a complicated double game—keeping German troops in Afghanistan to avoid censure from the United States and other Allies while ensuring German troops sustain minimal casualties to propitiate public opinion at home.

Thus any attempt to argue that casualties are not a key factor in the fall in German public support for the war runs into another "chicken and egg" problem—German casualties have been low precisely because fear of the public's reaction to casualties has caused German leaders to minimize the risk for German troops.

At the same time, German supporters of the war, such as Ulf Gartzke, have pointed out that German casualties need not necessarily quash support for the war if a strong and positive case for German involvement in Afghanistan were made.[306] In this respect, the Merkel Government seems simply to have assumed that the German public would be unwilling to pay the costs of war, without really trying to convince them otherwise. However, this has not been the case with all German Governments since 2001, as the next section will illustrate.

Casualties Plus Politics.

Elite Consensus. The German Government has enjoyed bipartisan consensus around its policy in Afghanistan since the first German troops were deployed in 2001—both the major parties, the CDU and the SPD, supported the dispatch of troops with only the former East German communist party, the PDS, opposed.[307] The bipartisan consensus in favor of a German force in the north of Afghanistan in a peacekeeping role has held firm through the change of Government from Schroeder's SPD to Merkel's CDU-SPD coalition and has even survived the fall of the coalition and the recent election campaign. However, there are signs that the SPD may break from the consensus—many grassroots activists desire a German pullout and, although the party leadership under Peter Struck is holding firm, competition from the openly anti-war die Linke party (an amalgam of leftist renegades from the SPD and former East German communists), is pressing the SPD to move to opposition to avoid a hemorrhage of support.[308] If and when the SPD begins to advocate a full German withdrawal, it would make sense to consider Germany as a country with elite dissensus. Before then, however, it would not. The anti-war die Linke under former SPD Finance Minister Oskar Lafontaine, although enjoying more popular support than Dennis Kucinich in the United States or George Galloway in the UK, is still a fringe party without a chance of attaining power.

Consequently, lack of elite consensus cannot explain the fall in support for the German mission.

Multilateralism. As we have seen, Germany has for many people in the United States, Britain, and elsewhere been the archetypal freerider in the Afghanistan conflict. Consequently, if multilateral burden sharing is an important part of the story, then German support for the war should hold up somewhat better than support in countries contributing more. Indeed, there is some evidence for this: the total fall in support in Germany has been lower than in most other countries in this assessment—although it starts from a much lower base. Unlike the French, the German Government has never acceded to British and American calls for greater participation in the south of Afghanistan, and it is unlikely, given the constellation of political forces within Germany, that they now will. However, if Germany were to begin to shoulder more of the burden in Afghanistan, and public support were to drop appreciably, this would constitute strong evidence that multilateral burden sharing is a key factor in Germany.

Principal Policy Objective. A priori it is not clear that a change in principal policy objective from restraint to counterinsurgency would have a major effect in Germany, which research such as Juhasz's has revealed to be skeptical of traditional uses of military force. Rather German voters may be more likely to support a mission that they perceive to be humanitarian peacekeeping than one that involves "hot" warfighting. This may explain the well-documented reluctance of

German leaders to refer to Afghanistan as a "war."[309] However, as Germany has, until now, done very little active warfighting in Afghanistan, it is difficult to ascribe falling German support to this factor in any significant degree.

Diminishing Prospects for Success. In spite of the small amount of polling data from Germany, we can see from Figure 18 that the trajectory of German support very roughly follows the same trend as in the other allied countries. After a relatively popular start the war begins to lose popularity in early 2007 and then achieves some stability thereafter with a small hardcore of supporters of approximately 30-40 percent of the population in favor and 50-60 percent against. This is consistent with an explanation in terms of diminishing prospects for success.

The Taliban resurgence in 2006 was picked up on by the German media as by other participating nations. *Die Zeit's* online edition in that year summarized the recent German media coverage of Afghanistan thus:

> Things will certainly get even worse. Recently large parts of Afghanistan have fallen back into the hands of the Taliban and al Qaeda. Should we wait until our troops come under fire again like the British in the south, and our aid workers can only operate from heavily fortified military compounds like in Kandahar? Such thoughts would easily occur to anyone who has regularly keeping himself informed about Afghanistan through the German media.[310]

Spiegel concurred:

> Altogether this is the worst year for Afghanistan since the US-led invasion in 2001. Since the beginning of the year around 3000 civilians have died, mostly bystanders.[311]

By 2007, German support for the war had begun to ebb, and the situation on the ground had worsened considerably, as the German news media ably reflected. For instance, the *Sueddeutsche Zeitung* reported in September of 2007:

> Taliban Advancing: in the last 6 weeks the Taliban are believed to have retaken control of numerous areas of southern Afghanistan. The affected areas include one-half of the localities from which American and Canadian troops had driven them a year ago.[312]

The *Berliner Zeitung* described 2007 as the "bloodiest year since the invasion,"[313] and the Sueddeutsche reported the Taliban to be "at the gates of Kabul."[314]

In short, German public opinion began to turn against the war at the point at which the war itself started to go seriously wrong for the Allies, a situation on the ground amply covered by the German press. Moreover, German opponents of the war, in addition to the expected arguments about the immorality of warfare (Lafontaine drew a moral equivalence between German air force bombers and terrorists),[315] have frequently used the argument that the war is pointless and bound to fail. SPD foreign affairs specialist Nils Annen, who reversed his 2001 support for the war, by 2009 claimed: "This form of war against terror is failing to produce positive results."[316]

Lafontaine himself also used the unwinnability argument, distorting the words of President Obama to do so:

> I demand that the Government withdraw the Bundeswehr from Afghanistan immediately. The German Army is being dragged ever deeper into a war

> which even President Obama recognizes is unwinnable.[317]

Likewise, in an interview with *Der Spiegel*, Lafontaine maintained the same theme:

> And when it comes to the issue of withdrawing our troops from Afghanistan, the SPD and the Greens will probably only come to their senses once U.S. President Barack Obama realizes that the war in Afghanistan cannot be won and withdraws his military.[318]

Within the SPD's anti-war faction, former cabinet Minister Renate Schmidt claimed that Germany "threatened to slide into a second Vietnam."[319]

Thus the trajectory of German public opinion on the war in Afghanistan, and the arguments used by opponents of the war, shows a strong impact of the progress of the war on the ground. Moreover, it is interesting that German support, like support in the UK or Canada, has stabilized at around 30-40 percent since 2007. This suggests that there is a core of "solid hawks" in the German public, although the term "hawk" should be used advisedly, since in the German case it would refer to voters who believe that the Bundeswehr should continue to be deployed in Afghanistan in any capacity at all. It does not refer to the existence of a 30-40 percent bloc of Germans in favor of aggressive war fighting in Afghanistan, whose existence we may doubt.

Afghanistan-Specific Theories.

Confused Rationale. The original decision to send German troops to Afghanistan in 2001 was taken by the then "Red-Green" coalition Government led by the SPD and the Green Party's Joschka Fischer. Fischer, a former 1960s radical and anti-war protestor, filled the role of Foreign Minister. At first glance it would seem unlikely that such a figure would champion or even support military intervention in Afghanistan in alliance with a Republican U.S. President. However, Fischer had been instrumental in persuading the German Greens to abandon their long-held pacifist beliefs in supporting German participation in the war in Kosovo.[320] Fischer became known internationally as a champion of "humanitarian interventionism"—the belief that it was morally justified for the West to intervene in the face of ethnic cleansing and genocide.[321] When NATO invoked Article V in the aftermath of 9/11 and Germany was called upon to provide troops in Afghanistan, Fischer naturally made the connection with Kosovo and humanitarian interventionism. As with Kosovo, German deployment outside NATO territory proved highly controversial within his own Green Party, so Fischer emerged as a passionate advocate of German involvement to help the Afghan people recover from Taliban oppression, develop their economy, and strengthen human rights:

> The following is clear: it isn't just about fighting terrorism over there, where it is currently a major threat, and destroying terror networks by military means. Rather it is above all about helping countries, helping people, slowly and gradually back to their feet—and this is a long and tedious task—and creating the conditions for a lasting peace.
>
> That is exactly the policy which the Federal Government (of Germany) has been following and will continue to follow. . . .

> In spite of all of the difficulties which we have outlined here, clear and visible achievements have been made. Two and a half million refugees have returned home. A minimum of stability has returned.[322]

Again at the Petersburg/Konigswinter Afghanistan donor's conference of 2002, Fischer made very similar points:

> It all depends on spreading human rights and better living conditions throughout the country. The danger of Islamist terror has not yet been banished. But security is only the first condition for a successful reconstruction strategy, which must encompass political structures, economics and social life. The Afghans now have a chance to create a peaceful social order which will endure. A social order which takes into consideration the diversity and multi-ethnic nature of the people and the universal human rights and democratic values of the community of nations. The important decisions must lie with the Afghans themselves. . . . Without international help they will not be able to do this job. . . . For Afghanistan is a particular task of the international community. The readiness to free the Afghan people from the frightful yoke of the Taliban is of central importance to the success of the international coalition against terrorism. It's about nothing less than the war of the civilized world against international terrorism, irrational fanaticism, and misanthropic criminality. That's why our common efforts must be successful. . . . With our help, President Karzai's regime must succeed in bringing peace, freedom and a fully human life to the people of Afghanistan. President Karzai, Chancellor Schroeder has said it well:- the International Community believes in a good future for your country. I appeal to you all to give all you can for this cause.[323]

Fischer's humanitarian sentiments were echoed by his boss, Gerhard Schroeder, on numerous occasions:

> For many months now, German soldiers have been fighting side by side with American troops in Afghanistan, once a haven and a logistical base for international terrorism. I am firmly convinced that we have no choice but to continue on in this common struggle, given the threat that global terrorism and al Qaeda pose to the international community.
>
> It would be tragic, both for the Afghan people and the international community, if this country were to relapse into tyranny or once more become a breeding ground for terrorists. We have a joint responsibility to prevent this, for it is in our common interest and in keeping with our common values.[324]

As Schroeder makes clear in the previous statement, and Fischer also stressed at points, the war in Afghanistan was not simply a pro-bono humanitarian intervention. German leaders, as their British and Canadian counterparts often did, claimed that the humanitarian and security rationales for the war were complementary—only an Afghanistan with a stable democratic government respectful of human rights would be a secure buffer against the Islamist terror threatening all Western nations. Schroeder's Defense Secretary, Peter Struck, played the security card more heavily when he claimed that "Germany is also being defended at the Hindu Kush."[325]

Thus the Schroeder Government did indeed offer a passionate and forthright defense of the Afghanistan deployment to the German people. Although security and humanitarian motives were intermingled in the rhetoric of the German leadership, the linkage between the two was made fairly clear. One may disagree with the proposition that a democratic Afghanistan is necessary for international security, but it would be unfair to maintain that Schroeder and Fischer were simply cycling through numerous and incoherent rationales.

Following the assumption of power by Angela Merkel's "Grand Coalition" of the conservative CDU and socialist SPD in 2005, German rhetoric on Afghanistan considerably toned down. Indeed, Merkel has rarely addressed the subject of Afghanistan or clearly defended the German deployment against domestic opposition, at least until the Kunduz incident of late 2009.[326] Rather, most of Merkel's public statements on the subject have been to defend the German deployment against American and British criticism that it has been insufficient.[327] The task of justifying the war was left to Merkel's Foreign Minister and rival Frank-Walter Steinmeier. Steinmeier used similar humanitarian rationales to Fischer, but curiously omitted much of the security rationale and added a further justification for the war—one which is also in evidence in the French debate—the importance of not letting one's allies down:

> Our engagement in Afghanistan is entering its 8th year! This is, I know, a real test of the international community's patience and staying power. And now of all times I say that the reasons we went into Afghanistan in 2001 are just as valid today as they were then! We gave our word to a nation blighted by thirty years of war and civil war. We realized from the start the magnitude of the task we'd taken on. And that's why—these days especially—we must honour our pledge. That's what we're now in the process of doing. The reality on the ground in Afghanistan has two faces. On the one hand we've achieved a great deal. Eighty-five percent of the population now live within reach of a doctor or hospital—a situation previously unknown. This is also due, by the way, to thousands of kilometres of newly constructed or repaired roads. The international community has cleared over half the mine-infested areas of

> the country. That, too, makes every Afghan's life safer. Economic recovery and reconstruction is making visible progress—not only in Kabul. Take Mazar-e-Sharif, for example. The provincial hospital we rehabilitated there is now the second largest teaching hospital in the country and every year trains 250 qualified nurses. We're talking about a country where only seven years ago people were stoned to death and music was banned. To all those who try to belittle our successes in Afghanistan, I say this: every bit of ground a farmer can once again cultivate, every child who can go to school, every new hospital, every kilometre of road—every one of these is a small victory for humanity. No one's being naive here. Of course this road we're on is stonier and longer than we'd all hoped. Every civilian casualty and every suicide bombing is a setback—and these setbacks are increasing, also in the north. Neither the international community nor the Afghan Government have yet effectively tackled corruption and opium trafficking. Terrorists continue to sow fear among local communities in the south and east, for the Afghan-Pakistan border is in practice unsecured.
>
> Ladies and gentlemen,
>
> That's the situation, the unvarnished truth. So what conclusions do we draw? Should we really quit when the going's tough, as some now demand? ***Is the job to be left to the Dutch, Norwegians, Poles and Finns—because we've shirked our responsibilities? If countries like us quit, that wouldn't just be a breach of the solidarity we've promised.*** Worse still, it would mean abandoning the goal for which we've been fighting for over six years. Our presence in Afghanistan is not and never was an end in itself. We had and have a clear goal. We want people in Afghanistan as soon as possible to take their country's future into their own hands and assume responsibility for its security.[328]

For Anja Dalgaard-Nielsen, the differing emphases of Steinmeier and Fischer represent the contrasting traditions of Germany's left and right with regard to security policy (though Steinmeier is a member of the SPD he could be seen as an inheritor of the more conservative security orientation of the party's right wing, represented in the Cold War by the likes of Helmut Schmidt). The German center-left, of whom Fischer is an exemplary representative, reacted to Germany's historical legacy in the 1950s and 1960s with the slogan "never again war" ("Nie wieder Krieg"). Over the course of the 1990s, however, many German leftists besides Fischer came to the conclusion that "never again Auschwitz" trumped "never again war" and that German military intervention was permissible if used for humanitarian purposes. The German center-right, by contrast, drew the opposing lesson "never again alone"—that is, that the use of force by Germany is acceptable if acting as part of the Western security community.[329]

The problem, however, with a rhetorical strategy based on appealing to solidarity with one's allies, as Ulf Gartzke might point out, is that it makes it easier for opponents of the war in Germany to claim that the real reason for the German deployment is to curry favor with other countries, specifically the United States—a trait we have already seen in Lafontaine's rhetoric. Given the relatively high levels of anti-American sentiment among some parts of the German public, as outlined in the introduction, this charge is dangerous for supporters of the mission. An argument more closely based on appeals to German self-interest and Germany's own security might have a better chance of arresting the decline in public support, according to this view.

Thus Germany presents an interesting case for the claim that inconsistent rationales for the war are part of the reason for the drop in support.

We have a clear contrast between the passionate advocacy of Fischer and other members of the Schroeder government and the more lukewarm rhetoric of the Merkel administration. The Merkel administration has also introduced a new rationale based around not alienating allies, which may actually prove counterproductive in selling the war to the German public.

Yet there are two problems with drawing any conclusions about the effect of rhetoric on public support for the war in Germany. First, although we have majority support for the war under the last polls taken on the issue when Schroeder was in power, followed by majority opposition under Merkel, there are too many confounding factors at work. The gap between the polls is several years, in the interim many things have changed in Afghanistan, most notably the prospects for the success of the mission on the ground, which this paper has suggested elsewhere is key to explaining the trajectory of British, U.S. and Canadian support. Second, it is possible that when a war is more politically damaging, political leaders will expend more time, energy, and imagination defending it than otherwise. One major reason why Fischer so often and so fervently defended the German deployment is because the war was very controversial within his own Green Party to the extent that it threatened to bring down the coalition of which he was Foreign Minister. The German deployment to Afghanistan has twice been put to a vote in the Bundestag. The first time was in 2001 under Schroeder's SPD-Green coalition. In this, Chancellor Schroeder was forced to trigger a vote of confidence so that if dissenting Green MPs voted against the Government in large enough numbers then an election would be triggered which the coalition was predicted to lose. Four Greens expressly voted to approve the deployment only to prevent the fall of the coalition. The deployment was approved by only two votes. [330]

Conversely, the second vote on the deployment, held in 2007 under Merkel's Government, passed by 442 votes to 96 with 32 abstentions.[331] With the pacifist-inclined Greens replaced by the conservative CDU-CSU in office, Merkel could be confident of a clear majority supporting the continuation of the deployment—provided German troops remained in the north of Afghanistan.

In other words, Fischer and Schroeder's relatively greater efforts to sell the deployment to the German people were actually the product of weak domestic position. Merkel, with a much greater margin of error, could afford to downplay the conflict. It is important to remember such considerations when seeking to attribute the fall in public support to insufficiently clear, energetic, or persuasive rhetoric from political leaders.

Since the victory of the CDU and its liberal partner, the FDP, in the German election, it has been assumed overseas that Merkel has a freer hand over Afghanistan. While this is true, there is little evidence that the current Chancellor herself is strongly in favor of the war—rather her public rhetorical strategy suggests her preference, even without the constraint of governing in coalition with a center-left party, would be for a continuation of a minimalist peacekeeping operation in northern Afghanistan principally to appease Germany's allies. The incoming Foreign Minister—the FDP's Guido Westerwelle—is seen as one of Germany's most ardent advocates of the Afghanistan operation.[332] Even his influence, however, is unlikely to lead to the kind of contribution at the sharp end from Germany that the Obama administration sought at the beginning of its term in office.[333] On the other hand, the recent incident in Kunduz, in which Bundeswehr soldiers were responsible for calling down an airstrike that killed over 100 civilians, has caused predictable soul-searching in Germany,[334] with recent opinion polls indicating only 27 percent of Germans still support the war, the lowest of any country in any time period in this analysis.[335]

Conclusion.

German public support for the war has arguably always been the most fragile of all the nations surveyed in this monograph. Of all of the participating countries at the outset of the conflict, Germany had the most troubled relationship with the use of force in international affairs. Moreover, Germany's history has made it easy for opponents of the war to demonize supporters—as seen in Lafontaine's "terrorists" comparison. It has also made it more difficult for supporters of the German mission such as Merkel to justify the mission more explicitly. In the German context, this will always raise the danger that someone to the left will raise the war-monger charge—if the SPD do not do so, then die Linke will wield the same charge against them. Thus, especially since Merkel's election, supporters of German involvement have been muted while opponents have been emboldened.

However, it would be wrong to say that Germany is not also responding to the same external stimuli as the Anglo-Saxons and the French. Indeed, the fall in support for the war in Germany since 2007 tracks very roughly the declining fortunes of the Allied campaign on the ground as do the drops in the United States, UK, Canada, Australia, and France. This shows in the reports of the German news media and in the rhetoric of the war's opponents. In other words, country specific factors such as Germany's particular attitudes toward the use of force, or anti-Americanism, are playing some role in the story, but the situation in Afghanistan is the key factor.

SUMMARY

It is clear from our examination of the trajectory of public support for the Afghanistan war in the United States, France, Germany, Australia, Canada, and Great Britain that multiple factors have gone into causing the increasing unpopularity of the conflict in each individual case. This should not be surprising—it is a common but naïve error in the social sciences to believe that social phenomena must have one and only one cause.[336] In the UK, the increasingly vocal opposition to the war in the news media, and covertly, and not so covertly, in the diplomatic service and the military has gone hand-in-hand with shifting rhetoric and mounting casualties to push public support down. In Canada, confused rhetoric again appears to have played a role alongside casualties in undermining the Harper government's case for Canadian intervention. The same is also true in France, where the multiple rationales used by Sarkozy and his allies have made the war appear to be waged at the behest of the United States, an unpopular image in a country whose public have a troublesome relationship with their American ally. In Germany, traditional pacifism has played a role; while in the United States, the switch from a straightforward denial mission in 2001 to a nation-building exercise played its part in undermining support. In Australia, however, it is hard to see what, other than diminishing prospects for the success of the mission, can have produced the drop in support—indeed, Australia is one of the strongest examples in favor of prospects of success being the most important driver of public opinion more generally. Moreover, as we have seen, diminishing prospects for success have impacted support in all cases.

However, if one holds to the view that political science is ultimately a practical discipline offering guidance to policymakers, a conclusion that many things have caused support to fall, while accurate, is also incomplete and unsatisfactory. For policymakers need to know the relative strengths of different factors, so that they can most effectively prioritize their time and attention. We need to be able to tease out the relative importance of different factors in order to make better policy. Qualitative methods offer us some ways of doing this.

One is to use a "most-different" research design.[337] If there are a row of light switches and all are set to off apart from one, but the light is still on, then one can be fairly confident that this is the switch that controls the light. Similarly, if a number of cases are observed in which all of the potentially important factors except one differ, but we observe the same result, then this is strong evidence that the one factor which is common to all cases is the most significant. In this case of Afghanistan, we observe different values for all of the factors which the academic, news media, and policy debate believes to be important with one exception—the progress of the Afghan war itself. Elite consensus, preexisting pacifist sentiment and/or anti-Americanism, casualties, traditions of interventionism, confused rhetoric, and relative burden all take on different values across the cases we have studied, as Figure 19 makes clear.

Country	*Elite Consensus*	*Participation in Iraq War*	*Shift in the rationale for war*	*Casualties*	*Prior anti-Americanism*	*Tradition of overseas interventionism/tolerance of force in international relations*	*Relative share of the burden*
Australia	High	Yes, until 2007	Low	Low	Low	High	Medium-High
Canada	Medium	No	High	High	Low	Medium	High
France	Medium	No	High	Low	High	High	Medium-High
Germany	Medium	No	High	Low	Medium	Low	Medium
United Kingdom	Medium	Yes, until 2009	High until 2009, low early 2009, high again late 2009	High	Low	High	High
United States	High	Yes	Medium until 2009, low since	High	N/A	High	High

Figure 19. Key Factors Across All Cases.

In no factor do we find uniformity across all countries. Do we see a common result—that is, the same trajectory of support across all the cases?

Subtracting the level of support in the latest poll from the level of support in the first poll might lead one to conclude that the percentage drop may differ by 5-10 percent between some countries, but it would be mistaken to draw such detailed inferences from the data we have. All polls come with a margin of error, and as we have seen in many countries, polls in the same country in the same month will give estimates of the degree of support for the war outside of one another' confidence margins—for example, the BBC and ITN polls in the UK in July 2009. In some of the countries involved, such as France, Germany, and Australia, polling has been sporadic and filled with gaps. Therefore, we cannot truly estimate the true degree of support in these countries with the same degree of precision as we can for states such as the

United States and Canada. Thus the figures we present for some countries are rather cruder estimations than they are for others. However, one thing is clear—the Afghanistan war has lost a large degree of support in all of the countries in this analysis, approximately 30-40 percent. The last country with majority support for the war is the United States. Moreover, the fall in U.S. support has been at least as great in magnitude as in other countries—the fact that U.S. approval was still above 50 percent only a few months ago is solely an artifact of the unprecedentedly high ratings the Afghan war enjoyed in the aftermath of 9/11. At the same time, idiosyncratic factors in each country have sometimes worked to keep support *higher* than it might otherwise have been—such as the low casualties suffered by the French, Germans, and Australians.

It follows that we have an approximately similar outcome in spite of variation in all of the most popular explanations except one—the course of the war itself. This suggests that although the trajectory of public support for the war may have been pushed one way or the other by idiosyncratic country-specific features in each individual case, the key driver in all of them is the deteriorating situation on the ground. This is the critical finding for policymakers. For some countries, such as Canada, the road to withdrawal is already irreversible. However, for others, especially the United States and Great Britain, it appears the best way for policymakers to stem the falling support for the war is to reverse the circumstances of the conflict on the ground in Afghanistan itself. If this cannot be done, and done in a way the public can observe, then this may indeed be the endgame for the West in Afghanistan.

BIBLIOGRAPHY

abcnews.go.com/Politics/Vote2008/story?page=1&id=5894022.

www.abc.net.au/news/indepth/solomons/.

www.abc.net.au/worldtoday/content/2006/s1670184.htm.

"A Brave New Dawn," *London Times* Editorial, December 8, 2004.

ac360.blogs.cnn.com/category/president-barack-obama/.

affaires-strategiques.iris-france.org/spip.php?article116.

"Afghanistan troops face long, difficult task: PM," AAP Newswire, Melbourne, Australia, April 10, 2007.

"Alliance of the Unwilling," *Time International*, April 2008.

www.ambafrance-ca.org/spip.php?article2404.

www.ambafrance-uk.org/French-presence-in-Afghanistan.html.

www.ambafrance-uk.org/Joint-declaration-on-Afghanistan.html.

www.amconmag.com/blog/exiting-afghanistan/.

Angus Reid Global Monitor.

archives.cnn.com/2001/US/09/11/congress.terrorism/.

www.army.gov.au/history/Historyofdawnsvc.htm.

atlanticreview.org/archives/1224-German-Soldiers-in-Afghanistan-Drinking-Instead-of-Fighting.html.

www.australia.gov.au/about-australia/our-government/australias-federation.

"Australia committed to Afghanistan conflict: Rudd," AAP, Sydney, Australia, October 15, 2008.

"Australian terror threat comes from Afghanistan, says Labor," AAP, Sydney, Australia, July 12, 2005.

www.auswaertiges-amt.de/diplo/de/Infoservice/Presse/Reden/Archiv/2002/021202-AfghanistanPetersberg.html.

www.auswaertiges-amt.de/diplo/en/Infoservice/Presse/Reden/2008/081007-Rede-BM-Afg-ISAF-BT.html.

www.awm.gov.au/.

Baum, Matthew, and Potter, Philip, "The Relationship between Mass Media, Public Opinion and Foreign Policy: Towards a Theoretical Synthesis," *Annual Review of Political Science*, Vol. 11, June 2008.

Bergen, Peter, "Winning the Good War: Why Afghanistan is not Obama's Vietnam," *Washington Monthly*, July 13, 2009.

Bermann, Paul, *Power and the Idealists: Or, the Passion of Joschka Fischer and Its Aftermath.* New York: Soft Skull Press, 2005.

www.berlinonline.de/berliner-zeitung/archiv/.bin/dump.fcgi/2007/1203/politik/0120/index.html.

Blair, Tony, *New Britain: My Vision of a Young Country*, Boulder, CO: Westview Press, 1997.

blogs.dailyrecord.co.uk/georgegalloway/2009/07/bring-in-helicopters-to-get-ou.html.

"British envoy says mission in Afghanistan is doomed, according to leaked memo," *The Times*, October 2, 2008.

"British Troops to Afghanistan," *London Times*, June 23, 2005.

cain.ulst.ac.uk/sutton/tables/Status.html.

"Cameron condemns 'scandal' of UK helicopter shortage in Afghanistan," *The Times*, July 13, 2009.

www.canberratimes.com.au/news/opinion/editorial/general/goals-clouded-in-the-fog-of-war/1472761.aspx?storypage=2.

www.canberratimes.com.au/news/world/world/general/britain-faces-questioning-on-losses-in-afghanistan/1568080.aspx?storypage=0.

www.casualtymonitor.org.

www.cbc.ca/canada/story/2008/03/13/motion-confidence.html.

www.cbc.ca/news/america/finaldata.pdf.

www.cbc.ca/news/background/afghanistan/casualties/list.html.

"Chirac says France will keep troops in Afghanistan," Agence France Presse, October 2005.

"Choosing which war to fight," *New York Times*, February 24, 2008.

www.cfr.org/publication/13114/kupchan.html.

www.cnn.com/2008/WORLD/europe/03/26/france.britain/index.html.

www.cnn.com/2009/WORLD/europe/03/11/france.sarkozy.nato/index.html.

www.collectionscanada.gc.ca.

www.commondreams.org/news2008/0110-10.htm.

Cotton, James, *East Timor, Australia and Regional Order*, London, UK: Routledge Curzon, 2004.

Coughlin, Con, *American Ally: Tony Blair and the War on Terror*, London, UK: HarperCollins Publishers, 2006.

www.ctv.ca/servlet/ArticleNews/story/CTVNews/20060517/nato_afghan_060517/20060517?hub=CTVNewsAt11.

www.dailymail.co.uk/news/article-1074489/MAX-HASTINGS-Afghanistan-Operation-Futility-unless-talk-Taliban.html.

Dalgaard-Nielsen, Anja, *Germany, Pacifism and Peace Enforcement*, Manchester, UK: Manchester University Press, 2006.

www.defence.gov.au/publications/lessons.pdf.

www.dfat.gov.au/GEO/afghanistan/afghanistan_country_brief.html.

"Digging in for Taliban Fight," AAP, April 20, 2006.

www.duke.edu/~grieco/Grieco_Second_Opinion.pdf.

www.dw-world.de/dw/article/0,,4000396,00.html.

Eichenberg, Richard, "Victory has many Friends: U.S. Public Opinion and the Use of Military Force 1981-2005," *International Security*, Vol. 30, No. 1, Summer 2005, pp. 140-177.

"Election Fears Said to Drive Merkel Policy on Afghanistan," *International Herald Tribune*, February 6, 2008.

www.eurasianet.org/departments/insight/articles/eav101708a.shtml.

Everts, Phillip and Isernia, Pierangelo, *Public Opinion and the International Use of Force*, New York: Routledge, 2001.

Everts, Phillip, "When the Going Gets Rough: Does the Public support the Use of Force?" *World Affairs*, 2000.

Feaver, Peter and Gelpi, Chris, *Choosing your Battles –American Civil-Military Relations and the Use of Force*, Princeton, NJ: Princeton University Press, 2004.

___________. *Paying the Human Costs of War*, unpublished manuscript.

Feaver, Peter; Gelpi, Chris, and Reifler, Jason, "Success Matters: Casualty Sensitivity and the War in Iraq," *International Security*, Winter 2005-06.

Fisk, Robert, "No End to the Centuries of Savagery in Afghanistan," *Belfast Telegraph*, November 17, 2008.

www.focus.de/politik/ausland/afghanistan-einsatz_aid_56848.html.

www.foxnews.com/politics/2009/02/18/commander-offers-grim-view-afghanistan/.

Friedman, Thomas L, "Afghanistan's Future is in the Hands of U.S. Soldiers who refuse to quit," *San Jose Mercury*, July 22, 2009.

www.frontnational.com/communique_detail.php?id=1762.

Gartner, Scott and Segura, Gary, "Casualties and Public Opinion," *Journal of Conflict Resolution*, Vol. 42, No. 3, pp. 278-300.

George, Alexander L., and Bennett, Andrew, *Case Studies and Theory Development in the Social Sciences*, Cambridge, MA: MIT Press, 2005.

greens.org.au/node/4982.

Gross-Stein, Janice, *The Unexpected War: Canada in Kandahar*, Toronto, Canada: Viking Press, 2007.

www.gruene-bundestag.de/cms/bundestagsreden/dok/18/18471.joschka_fischer_afghanistaneinsatz.html.

www.guardian.co.uk/.

Gyngell, Allan and Wesley, Michael, *Making Australian Foreign Policy*, Cambridge UK: Cambridge University Press, 2003.

hebdo.parti-socialiste.fr/2008/04/02/1226/.

www.hks.harvard.edu/news-events/news/press-releases/stewart-carr-center.

Hopkirk, Peter, *The Great Game, the Struggle for Empire in Central Asia*, Oxford, UK: Oxford University Press, 2001.

Horn, Bernd, *No Ordinary Men: Special Forces Missions in Afghanistan*, Toronto, Canada: Dundum Press, 2009.

"Howard warns of dangers for diggers," AAP Newswire, Sydney, Australia, July 9, 2007.

Howard, Sir Michael, "What's in a Name? How to Fight Terrorism," *Foreign Affairs*, January-February 2002, pp. 8-13.

icasualties.org/.

ipsnews.net/news.asp?idnews=38512.

Jenkins, Simon, "Fall Back Men! Afghanistan is a nasty war we can never win," *The Times*, February 3 2008.

Jentleson, Bruce, "The Pretty Prudent Public: Post-Vietnam American Opinion on the Use of Force," *International Studies Quarterly*, Vol. 36, No. 1, 1994, pp. 49-74.

Jentleson, Bruce, and Britton, Rebecca L, "Still Pretty Prudent: Post-Cold War American Public Opinion on the Use of Force," *Journal of Conflict Resolution*, Vol. 42, No. 4, pp. 395-417.

Kampfner, John, *Blair's Wars*, London, UK: Free Press, 2003.

kingsofwar.wordpress.com/2008/06/08/an-army-falling-apart/.

Kipling, Rudyard, *War Stories and Poems*, Oxford, UK: Oxford University Press, 1999.

Kull, Stephen, and Destler, I. M., *Misreading the Public – The Myth of a New Isolationism*, Washington, DC: The Brookings Institution Press, 1999.

Larson, Eric V., *Casualties and Consensus – The Historical Role of Casualties in Domestic Support for U.S. Military Interventions*, Santa Monica, CA: The RAND Corporation, 1996.

www.lemonde.fr/cgibin/ACHATS/acheter.cgi?offre=ARCHIVES&type_item=ART_ARCH_30J&objet_id=1000476.

www.lepoint.fr/actualites-monde/2008-10-06/un-general-britannique-predit-un-echec-militaire-en-afghanistan/1648/0/279806.

The Lowy Institute, Sydney, Australia.

lyceum.anu.edu.au/wpntent/blogs/3/uploads//ANU%20Poll%20Defence%20Report%201.pdf.

www.mod.uk/DefenceInternet/DefenceNews/MilitaryOperations/JohnReidbritishTaskForceHasAVitalJobToDoInSouthernAfghanistan.html.

www.montesquieu-institute.eu/9353000/1/j9vvhfxcd6p0lcl/vgnldm4wfwze?ctx=vg09llo6puxp.

Mueller, John, "Trends in American Public Support for the Wars in Korea and Vietnam," *American Political Science Review*, June 1971, pp. 358-376.

www.naval-history.net/NAVAL1982FALKLANDS.htm.

network.nationalpost.com/np/blogs/fullcomment/archive/2009/07/13/poppycock-politics-why-it-s-legal-to-grow-opium-in-england-but-not-in-afghanistan.aspx.

news.bbc.co.uk/2/hi/uk_news/8141591.stm.

newsweek.washingtonpost.com/postglobal/fareed_zakaria/2009/02/four_keys_to_success_in_afghan.html.

news.smh.com.au/breaking-news-world/us-troops-militants-die-in-afghan-clash-20090725-dwet.html.

www.newyorker.com/online/blogs/georgepacker/2008/11/kilcullen-on-af.html.

Nincic, Miroslav and Lepgold, Joseph, *Being Useful: Policy Relevance and International Relations Theory*, Ann Arbor, MI: University of Michigan, 2000.

nobelprize.org/nobel_prizes/peace/laureates/1957/pearson-bio.html.

Norton-Taylor, Richard, "UK's Afghan Mission at a Turning Point, says Browne," *Guardian*, August 16, 2007.

www.nytimes.com/2008/06/30/world/europe/30iht-politicus.1.14095817.html.

www.nytimes.com/2009/01/20/us/politics/20text-obama.html.

www.nytimes.com/2001/11/17/world/pressing-greens-german-leader-wins-historic-vote-sending-troops-afghanistan.html.

www.operationgranby.com/.

Parris, Matthew, "Enough, time to pack up and leave," *The Times*, February 2, 2008.

Patterson, Kevin, and Warren, Jane, *Outside the Wire: the War for Afghanistan in the Words of its Participants*, Toronto, Canada: Random House, 2007.

Pew Global Research.

www.presseportal.de/pm/41150/1444504/die_linke.

www.publications.parliament.uk/pa/cm200809/cmhansrd/cm090716/debindx/90716-x.htm.

"Playing Politics with Afghanistan," Editorial, *Globe and Mail*, September 11, 2008.

"PM, Nelson announce long-awaited Afghan deployment," AAP, Sydney, Australia, April 10, 2007.

www.pbs.org/newshour/bb/politics/jan-june09/obamainterview_02-27.html.

ProQuest.

www.publications.parliament.uk/pa/cm200809/cmhansrd/cm090716/debtext/90716-0011.htm.

Rashid, Ahmed, *Descent into Chaos: The United States and the Failure of Nation Building in Afghanistan*. New York: Viking Press, 2008.

"Remarks by the President on a new strategy for Afghanistan and Pakistan," Washington, DC: The White House, Office of the Press Secretary, March 29, 2009.

www.reuters.com/article/asiaCrisis/idUSL231001602.

www.reuters.com/article/featuredCrisis/idUSN12426542.

www.ronpaul.com/2009-06-30/ron-paul-republicans-should-oppose-perpetual-war-and-unsound-money/.

The Roper Data Center, University of Connecticut, Storrs, CT.

Roselle, Laura, *Media and the Politics of Failure: Great Powers, Communication Strategies and Military Defeats*, New York: Palgrave MacMilan, 2006.

"Sarkozy resolute on Afghanistan despite the deaths of 10 French soldiers," *Christian Science Monitor*, August 20, 2008.

"SAS death won't change Govt resolve on terror, says PM," AAP, Sydney, Australia, October 26 2007.

Schroeder, Gerhard, "Germany will share the burden in Iraq," *New York Times*, September 2003.

Shawcross, William, *Deliver us from Evil: Peacekeepers, Warlords and a World of Endless Conflict*, New York: Simon & Schuster, 2000.

Sheridan, Greg, *The Partnership: The Inside Story of the US-Australian Alliance Under Bush and Howard*, Sydney, Australia: University of New South Wales Press, 2006.

slate.msn.com/?id=2059487.

Speech by Jacques Chirac, President of the French Republic, at the International Conference on Drug Routes, Paris, France, Thursday 22 May, 2003.

www.spiegel.de/politik/ausland/0,1518,445141,00.html.

www.spiegel.de/international/europe/0,1518,479838,00.html.

www.spiegel.de/international/germany/0,1518,624880,00.html.

Statement to the House of Commons following the G8 by the Prime Minister Rt. Hon. Gordon Brown, MP, London, UK, July 13, 2009.

Stewart, Rory, "Afghanistan: a war we cannot win," *The Daily Telegraph*, July 10, 2009.

Strachan, Hew, *Big Wars and Small Wars, the British Army and the Lessons of Warfare in the 20 Century*, London, UK: Routledge, 2006.

www.sueddeutsche.de/politik/277/417043/text/.

Taylor, Peter, *Brits: the War against the IRA*, London, UK: Bloomsbury, 2002.

www.telegraph.co.uk/news/worldnews/australiaandthepacific/australia/5243123/Australia-to-send-more-troops-to-Afghanistan.html.

www.telegraph.co.uk/news/worldnews/asia/afghanistan/2585674/Taliban-kill-10-French-paratroopers-in-Afghanistan-ambush.html.

tempsreel.nouvelobs.com/actualites/politique/20080922.OBS2254/debat_sur_lafghanistan__le.

tempsreel.nouvelobs.com/depeches/politique/20080820.FAP1530/patrick_devedjian_critique_lattitude_du_ps_sur_lafghani.htm.

www.the-american-interest.com/article.cfm?piece=617.

www.theage.com.au.

www.theaustralian.news.com.au.

www.thesun.co.uk/sol/homepage/news/article577388.ece.

"The Murderous Fruits of Neglect: Afghanistan," *The Independent*, September 26, 2006.

www.time.com/time/world/article/0,8599,1909254-5,00.html.

www.timesonline.co.uk/tol/news/world/iraq/article3405928.ece.

Transatlantic Trends Survey, June 2004.

uk.reuters.com/article/idUKL411664020080904.

www.u-m-p.org/site/index.php/ump/l_ump/notre_histoire.

Volpe, Peter, *Understanding Military Intervention in the Post-Cold War era*, Unpublished Ph.D. Dissertation, Duke University, 2004.

Walters, Patrick, "Out of our depth," *The Australian*, May 3, 2008.

"War on Terror will not end soon, PM says," AAP, Sydney, Australia, February 25, 2006.

www.washingtonpost.com/wp-dyn/content/article/2007/04/18/AR2007041802245.html.

www.washingtonpost.com/wp-dyn/articles/A60915-2004Nov18.html.

www.watoday.com.au/opinion/up-the-khyber-but-with-a-paddle-20090430-aokm.html?page=-1.

Wattie, Chris, *Contact Charlie: The Canadian Army, the Taliban and the Battle that saved Afghanistan*, Toronto, Canada: Key Porter Books, 2008.

"We can't defeat Taliban, says Brigadier Mark Carleton-Smith," *The Times*, October 6, 2008.

Weekly Compilation of Presidential Documents.

www.weeklystandard.com/weblogs/TWSFP/2008/06/germany_to_send_1000_more_troo_1.asp.

www.whitehouse.gov.

Mackiewicz-Wolfe, Wojteck, *Winning the War of Words: Selling the War on Terror from Afghanistan to Iraq*, Westport, CT: Praeger Publishers, 2008.

www.worldpublicopinion.org/pipa/articles/international_security_bt/535.php?lb=btot&pnt=535&nid=&id=.

yglesias.thinkprogress.org/archives/2009/07/a-winnable-war-in-afghanistan.php.

yglesias.thinkprogress.org/archives/2008/08/the_trouble_with_pro_american.php.

Zakaria, Fareed. "A Turnaround Strategy," *Newsweek*, January 31, 2009.

www.zeit.de/online/2006/46/Afghanistan-Analyse.

ENDNOTES

1. Gallup/CNN/USA Today Poll, Storrs, CT: University of Connecticut, Roper Data Center, March 2002.

2. Pew Research Center Poll, Storrs, CT: University of Connecticut, Roper Data Center, September 2008; Pew Global Attitudes Survey, Storrs, CT: University of Connecticut, Roper Data Center, April 2008.

3. CNN Opinion Research Poll, Storrs, CT: University of Connecticut, Roper Data Center, July 2008.

4. Pew Global Research Poll, in association with the *International Herald Tribune* and the Council on Foreign Relations, April 2002, available from *www.timesonline.co.uk/tol/news/politics/article4138809.ece*.

5. Ekos Research Associates Poll, March 2006, source *Angus Reid Global Monitor*; Ekos Research Associates Poll, November 2006, source *Angus Reid Global Monitor*.

6. Strategic Counsel Poll, September 2008, available from *www.thestrategiccounsel.com/our_news/polls/Pre-Election Baseline - Sep 1 (with second choice).pdf*.

7. Dennis Shanahan, "The Third Howard Government," *The Australian*, March 29, 2002.

8. Lowy Institute Poll, Australia and the World, July 2008, available from *www.lowyinstitute.org/Publication.asp?pid=895*.

9. CSA/Le Croix Poll, October 2001, source: *Angus Reid Global Data Monitor*, available from *www.ropercenter.uconn.edu/*.

10. BVA/L'Express Poll, September 2008, source: *Angus Reid Global Data Monitor*, available from *www.csa-tmo.fr/fra/dataset/data2001/opi20011030a.htm*.

11. Pew Global Poll, April 2002, available from *people-press.org/report/165/what-the-world-thinks-in-2002*.

12. Infratest-Dimap Poll, December 2009, source: *Angus Reid Global Data Monitor,* available from *www.angus-reid.com/polls/view/french_want_soldiers_out_of_afghanistan/.*

13. John Mueller, "Trends in American Public Support for the Wars in Korea and Vietnam," *American Political Science Review,* June 1971, p. 366.

14. Scott Gartner and Gary Segura, "War, Casualties and Public Opinion," *Journal of Conflict Resolution,* Vol. 42, No. 3, p. 279.

15. Eric Larson, *Casualties and Consensus,* Santa Monica, CA: The RAND Corporation, 1996, p. 78.

16. Bruce Jentleson, "The Pretty Prudent Public: Post-Vietnam American Opinion on the Use of Force," *International Studies Quarterly,* Vol. 36, No 1., p. 54.

17. Steven Kull and I. M. Destler, *Misreading the Public—The Myth of a New Isolationism,* Washington, DC: The Brookings Institute, 1999, p. 101.

18. Joseph Grieco, Chris Gelpi, Peter Feaver, and Jason Reifler, "Let's Get a Second Opinion: Allies, the UN and US Public Opinion," *International Studies Quarterly,* 2009, available from *iicas.ucsd.edu/papers/PIA/gelpi_paper.pdf.*

19. Kull and Destler, pp. 111, 253.

20. Available from *www.un.org/News/Press/docs/2001/sc7248.doc.htm.*

21. "Nicholas Sarkozy to bolster force in Afghanistan with 1,000 extra troops," *Times,* March 22, 2008; available from *www.cfr.org/publication/13114/kupchan.html.*

22. Peter Feaver and Christopher Gelpi, "Paying the Human Costs of War," Princeton, NJ: Princeton University Press, 2009, p. 17.

23. *Ibid.,* p. 23.

24. Helene Cooper, "Choosing which war to fight," *New York Times*, February 24, 2008; Barack Obama, speech at Cape Girardeau, Mississippi, May 13, 2008, available from *www.politifact.com/truth-o-meter/statements/489/*.

25. Janice Gross-Stein, *The Unexpected War: Canada in Kandahar*, Toronto, Canada: Viking Press, 2007, p. 290; Michael Portillo, "Just One Clear Aim will save British Lives, September 6, 2009, available from *www.timesonline.co.uk/tol/comment/columnists/guest_contributors/article6823315.ece*; also see *news.bbc.co.uk/2/hi/uk_news/7443195.stm*; Independent Panel on Canada's Future Role in Afghanistan, January 2008, p. 24, available from *epe.lac-bac.gc.ca/100/200/301/pco-bcp/commissions-ef/independent_panel_afghanistan-ef/final_report-e/pdf/Afghan_Report_web_e.pdf*; Author's interview with Janice Gross-Stein, August 17, 2009.

26. William Shawcross, *Deliver us from Evil: Peacekeepers, Warlords and a World of Endless Conflict*, New York: Touchstone, 2000, p. 135.

27. Steven Kull and Clay Ramsay, "American Public Attitudes," in Philip Everts and Pierangelo Isernia, eds., *Public Opinion and the International Use of Force*, New York: Routledge, 2001, pp. 213-214.

28. *Ibid.*, p. 215.

29. *Ibid.*, p. 217.

30. *Ibid.*, pp. 220-221.

31. *Ibid.*, pp. 217-218.

32. *Ibid.*, p. 223.

33. *Ibid.*, pp. 255-256.

34. *Ibid.*, p. 215.

35. Available from *icasualties.org/OEF/ByNationality.aspx*.

36. Available from *archives.cnn.com/2001/US/09/11/congress.terrorism/*.

37. Available from *www.cfr.org/publication.html?id=6576.*

38. Available from *abcnews.go.com/Politics/Vote2008/story?page=1&id=5894022.*

39. Available from *www.the-american-interest.com/article.cfm?piece=617.*

40. Available from *www.commondreams.org/news2008/0110-10.htm.*

41. Available from *www.ronpaul.com/2009-06-30/ron-paul-republicans-should-oppose-perpetual-war-and-unsound-money/.*

42. "Top Democrat not ready to embrace Afghan troop surge," Associated Free Press, October 14, 2009; "Pelosi Questions Afghan Surge," available from *www.msnbc.msn.com/id/32782622.*

43. Available from *www.npr.org/templates/story/story.php?storyId=113130422.*

44. Fareed Zakaria, "A Turnaround Strategy," *Newsweek*, January 31, 2009, available from *www.newsweek.com/id/182651.*

45. Peter Bergen, "Winning the Good War: Why Afghanistan is not Obama's Vietnam," *Washington Monthly*, July 13, 2009.

46. Thomas L Friedman, "Afghanistan's Future is in the Hands of U.S. soldiers who refuse to quit," *San Jose Mercury*, July 22, 2009.

47. Bergen.

48. Available from *yglesias.thinkprogress.org/archives/2009/07/a-winnable-war-in-afghanistan.php.*

49. Available from *www.huffingtonpost.com/2009/09/01/george-will-afghanistan-c_n_274344.html.*

50. CNN/Opinion Research Corporation Poll March 2007; Pew Global Research Poll, April 2007.

51. "A Fight in Afghanistan: The War is Far from over. Can it be won by NATO?" *The Washington Post*, May 24, 2006.

52. CNN/Opinion Research Poll, August 2006.

53. Transatlantic Trends Survey, June 2004.

54. "Misunderstanding Afghanistan," *The Washington Post*, December 17, 2006. Includes the *Newsweek*, *Los Angeles Times*, and Kerry quotes.

55. "NATO not winning in Afghanistan, Report Says," *The Washington Post*, January 31, 2008.

56. "Taliban, al-Qaeda Resurge in Afghanistan, CIA says," *The Washington Post*, November 16, 2007; CNN/Opinion Research Poll, January 2007, source: Roper Data Center.

57. Available from *www.foxnews.com/politics/2009/02/18/commander-offers-grim-view-afghanistan/*.

58. Available from *www.nytimes.com/2009/01/20/us/politics/20text-obama.html*.

59. Available from *www.foxnews.com/story/0,2933,541725,00.html*.

60. *Available from www.washingtonpost.com/wp-dyn/content/article/2009/09/20/AR2009092002920.html*.

61. Gallup/*USA Today* Poll, February 2009.

62. CNN/Opinion Research Corporation Poll, December 2009.

63. Pew Research Center for People and the Press.

64. ABC/*The Washington Times* Poll, March 2009—Question "Do you think the USA made a mistake in sending military forces to Afghanistan or no?" 56 percent answered "No." Source: Roper Data Center.

65. Pew News Interest Poll, December 2006—Question "Do you think the USA made the right decision or the wrong decision in using military force in Afghanistan?" 63 percent answered "the right decision." Source: Roper Data Center.

66. Gallup/*USA Today*/CNN Poll, June 2004- same question as in 2008 Gallup poll, 72 percent answered "No." Source: Roper Data Center.

67. In July 2004, 72 percent believed the war in Afghanistan was not a mistake. This had fallen only to 69 percent by January 2006. No margin of error was provided so it is not possible to see if this difference is statistically significant. But even if it is statistically significant, it is not substantively significant.

68. Mark Silva, "Bush, Karzai: Afghans Gain Ground against terror, drugs; Leaders, Delegations meet at Camp David," Knight Rider Tribune Business News, August 7, 2007.

69. George W Bush, "Afghanistan, Pakistan and the Global War on Terror," *The Officer*, November 2006, p. 45.

70. Remarks to the American Enterprise Institute for Public Policy Research, February 19, 2007, Weekly Compilation of Presidential Documents.

71. Address to Veterans of Foreign Wars, National Convention, Orlando, FL, August 20, 2008, available from *www.whitehouse.gov/infocus/nationalsecurity/*.

72. Remarks Following a Briefing by Provincial Reconstruction Team Commanders, George W Bush, Weekly Compilation of Presidential Documents, March 17, 2008.

73. President George W Bush, Weekly Radio Address, October 2, 2006.

74. George W Bush delivers remarks on terrorism, Political Transcript Wire, September 29, 2006.

75. Available from *www.pbs.org/newshour/bb/politics/jan-june09/obamainterview_02-27.html*.

76. Remarks by the President on a new strategy for Afghanistan and Pakistan, Washington, DC: The White House, Office of the Press Secretary, March 29, 2009.

77. Available from *ac360.blogs.cnn.com/category/president-barack-obama/.*

78. Available from *newsweek.washingtonpost.com/postglobal/fareed_zakaria/2009/02/four_keys_to_success_in_afghan.html.*

79. Interview with Janice Gross-Stein by the author, August 17, 2009.

80. Available from *blogs.abcnews.com/politicalpunch/2009/04/president-oba-4.html.*

81. Available from *shadow.foreignpolicy.com/posts/2009/12/03/what_the_afghan_policy_rollout_tells_us_about_obamas_domestic_agenda.*

82. Available from *i2.cdn.turner.com/cnn/2009/images/12/04/rel18a.pdf.*

83. Available from *atwar.blogs.nytimes.com/2009/11/04/going-tribal-in-afghanistan/.*

84. Available from *www.australia.gov.au/about-australia/our-government/australias-federation.*

85. Available from *www.army.gov.au/history/Historyofdawnsvc.htm.*

86. Available from *www.awm.gov.au/commemoration/anzac/anzac_tradition.asp.*

87. Mel Gibson's 1981 movie, Galipolli, and Paul Hogan's 1985 television series, ANZACs, are examples of this strain in Australian popular culture.

88. Available from *www.awm.gov.au/atwar/index/korea.asp.*

89. Available from *www.awm.gov.au/atwar/vietnam.asp.*

90. Available from *www.awm.gov.au/atwar/gulf.asp.*

91. Available from *www.defence.gov.au/publications/lessons.pdf.*

92. James Cotton, *East Timor, Australia and Regional Order*, London, UK: Routledge Curzon, 2004, p. 71.

93. Available from *www.abc.net.au/news/indepth/solomons/.*

94. *Sydney Morning Herald* Poll, September 14, 1999.

95. Available from *yglesias.thinkprogress.org/archives/2008/08/the_trouble_with_pro_american.php.*

96. Available from *www.cbc.ca/news/america/finaldata.pdf.*

97. Greg Sheridan, *The Partnership: The Inside Story of the U.S.-Australian Alliance*, Sydney, Australia: University of New South Wales, 2006, p. 42.

98. Available from *icasualties.org/OEF/ByNationality.aspx.*

99. Available from *www.theaustralian.news.com.au/story/0,25197,25964265-601,00.html.*

100. Available from *www.economist.com/displayStory.cfm?story_id=13279199.*

101. Available from *www.dfat.gov.au/GEO/afghanistan/afghanistan_country_brief.html.*

102. Available from *pewglobal.org/reports/display.php?ReportID=260.*

103. Available from *lyceum.anu.edu.au/wp-content/blogs/3/uploads//ANU%20Poll%20Defence%20Report%201.pdf.*

104. Lowy Institute Poll, Australia and the World, June 2008.

105. *Ibid.*

106. Essential Research Poll, April 2009, source: *Angus Reid Global Data Monitor.*

107. Newspoll/The Australian Poll, April 2009.

108. Available from *www.defence.gov.au/ADC/docs/Publications/Strategic%20Management%20Papers/Caughey%20Strat%20Mgt%20%20%2008%20designed.pdf*; also available from *www.dnd.ca/site/pri/1/index-eng.asp.*

109. Sheridan, p. 43.

110. "Australia in Afghanistan for the long haul: Rudd," AAP General News Wire, October 26, 2007.

111. Available from *greens.org.au/node/4982.*

112. Available from *www1.voanews.com/english/news/a-13-2009-07-20-voa15-68789577.html.*

113. Available from *www.newyorker.com/online/blogs/georgepacker/2008/11/kilcullen-on-af.html.*

114. Available from *www.theaustralian.news.com.au/story/0,25197,23175015-25837,00.html.*

115. Available from *www.watoday.com.au/opinion/up-the-khyber-but-with-a-paddle-20090430-aokm.html?page=-1.*

116. Available from *www.canberratimes.com.au/news/opinion/editorial/general/goals-clouded-in-the-fog-of-war/1472761.aspx?storypage=2.*

117. Available from *www.telegraph.co.uk/news/worldnews/australiaandthepacific/australia/5243123/Australia-to-send-more-troops-to-Afghanistan.html.*

118. Essential Research Poll, May 2009, source *Angus Reid Global Data Monitor.*

119. Available from *www.abc.net.au/worldtoday/content/2006/ s1670184.htm.*

120. Available from *www.canberratimes.com.au/news/world/ world/general/britain-faces-questioning-on-losses-in-afghanistan/1568080.aspx?storypage=0*; also available from *www. theaustralian.news.com.au/story/0,25197,24386218-25837,00.html.*

121. Available from *news.smh.com.au/breaking-news-world/us-troops-militants-die-in-afghan-clash-20090725-dwet.html.*

122. Available *from www.abc.net.au/am/content/2008/s2150591. htm.*

123. Available from *www.guardian.co.uk/world/2007/nov/30/usa. iraq.*

124. Available from *www.canberratimes.com.au/news/opinion /editorial/general/goals-clouded-in-the-fog-of-war/1472761. aspx?storypage=4.*

125. Lowy Institute Poll, "Australia and the World," July 2008, p. 12.

126. "Digging in for Taliban Fight," AAP, April 20, 2006.

127. "Howard warns of dangers for diggers," AAP Newswire, Sydney, Australia, July 9, 2007.

128. "Afghanistan troops face long, difficult task: PM," AAP Newswire, Melbourne, Australia, April 10, 2007.

129. "SAS death won't change Govt resolve on terror, says PM," AAP, Sydney, Australia, October 26, 2007.

130. "War on Terror will not end soon, PM says," AAP, Sydney, Australia, February 25, 2006.

131. "PM, Nelson announce long-awaited Afghan deployment," AAP, Sydney, Australia, April 10, 2007.

132. "Australia committed to Afghanistan conflict: Rudd," AAP, Sydney, Australia, October 15, 2008.

133. Patrick Walters, "Out of our depth," *The Australian*, May 3, 2008.

134. "Australian terror threat comes from Afghanistan, says Labor," AAP, Sydney, Australia, July 12, 2005.

135. Peter Hopkirk, *The Great Game, the Struggle for Empire in Central Asia*, Oxford, UK: Oxford University Press, 2001.

136. Rudyard Kipling, "The Young British Soldier," *War Stories and Poems*, Oxford, UK: Oxford University Press, 1999.

137. Hew Strachan, *Big Wars and Small Wars, the British Army and the Lessons of Warfare in the 20 Century*, London, UK: Routledge, 2006.

138. Peter Taylor, *Brits: the War against the IRA*, London, UK: Bloomsbury, 2002, available from *cain.ulst.ac.uk/sutton/tables/Status.html*.

139. Available from *www.naval-history.net/NAVAL1982FALKLANDS.htm*.

140. Available from *www.operationgranby.com/*.

141. Tony Blair, *New Britain: My Vision of a Young Country*, Boulder, CO: Westview Press, 1997.

142. John Kampfner, *Blair's Wars*, London, UK: Free Press, 2003, p. i.

143. Pew Global Attitudes Project, June 2007.

144. CNN Poll, April 22-25, 1999, cited in Everts and Isernia, p. 236.

145. *Ibid.*, pp. 255-256.

146. Peter Volpe, "Understanding Military Intervention in the Post-Cold War era," Unpublished Ph.D. Dissertation, Duke University, 2004, pp. 384-388.

147. Available from *www.cbc.ca/news/america/finaldata.pdf.*

148. Pew Global Attitudes Project, December 18, 2008.

149. Available from *www.worldpublicopinion.org/pipa/articles/international_security_bt/535.php?lb=btot&pnt=535&nid=&id=.*

150. Available from *www.cbc.ca/news/america/finaldata.pdf.*

151. Available from *icasualties.org/OEF/ByNationality.aspx.*

152. Pew Global Attitudes Project, April 17, 2002.

153. BBC/ICM Poll, "Press Release," October 6, 2009.

154. "Cameron condemns 'scandal' of UK helicopter shortage in Afghanistan," *The Times*, July 13, 2009.

155. Available from *news.bbc.co.uk/2/hi/uk_news/8141591.stml.* Recent reports have claimed that the Conservatives are looking for an "exit strategy" for Afghanistan, but it is clear from reading the words of Defense Spokesman Fox that this is not the case. He stated, "Setting artificial timetables for political reasons runs the risk of saying to our enemies 'if you outlast us we will run'." Available from *www.guardian.co.uk/politics/2009/aug/23/liam-fox-afghanistan-troops-conservatives.*

156. Available from *www.publications.parliament.uk/pa/cm200809/cmhansrd/cm090716/debindx/90716-x.htm.*

157. Available from *blogs.dailyrecord.co.uk/georgegalloway/2009/07/bring-in-helicopters-to-get-ou.html.*

158. Available from *www.guardian.co.uk/commentisfree/2009/nov/03/afghanistan-terror-taliban-al-qaida.*

159. Robert Fisk, "No End to the Centuries of Savagery in Afghanistan," *Belfast Telegraph*, November 17, 2008.

160. Sir Michael Howard, "What's in a Name? How to Fight Terrorism," *Foreign Affairs*, January-February 2002, pp. 8-13.

161. Simon Jenkins, "Fall Back Men! Afghanistan is a nasty war we can never win," *The Times*, February 3, 2008.

162. Matthew Parris, "Enough, time to pack up and leave," *The Times*, February 2, 2008.

163. Max Hastings, "Afghanistan is Operation Futility unless we talk to the Taliban," available from *www.dailymail.co.uk/news/article-1074489/MAX-HASTINGS-Afghanistan-Operation-Futility-unless-talk-Taliban.html*.

164. Rory Stewart, "Afghanistan: a war we cannot win," *The Daily Telegraph*, July 10, 2009.

165. "British envoy says mission in Afghanistan is doomed, according to leaked memo," *The Times*, October 2, 2008.

166. "We can't defeat Taliban, says Brigadier Mark Carleton-Smith," *The Times*, October 6, 2008.

167. Available from *www.guardian.co.uk/world/2008/oct/06/afghanistan.military*.

168. Available from *www.timesonline.co.uk/tol/news/uk/article4862254.ece*.

169. Available from *www.hks.harvard.edu/news-events/news/press-releases/stewart-carr-center*.

170. Available from *www.guardian.co.uk/commentisfree/2006/nov/22/comment.politics1*.

171. Available from *www.guardian.co.uk/world/cartoon/2009/feb/19/afghanistan-obama-troops*.

172. Stewart.

173. "A Brave New Dawn," *London Times* Editorial, December 8, 2004.

174. "British Troops to Afghanistan," *London Times*, June 23, 2005.

175. "The Murderous Fruits of Neglect: Afghanistan," *The Independent*, September 26, 2006.

176. ICM Poll, November 2008.

177. Available from *populuslimited.com/uploads/download_pdf-110709-ITN-News-Afghanistan-Survey.pdf*; also available from *www.guardian.co.uk/uk/2009/jul/13/afghanistan-war-poll-public-support*.

178. Angus Reid Polls, "Britain, Canada Differ from U.S. on Afghan War," July 23, 2009. Poll in three nations suggests British support for the war is now at 39 percent, available from *www.angus-reid.com/polls/view/britain_canada_differ_from_us_on_afghan_war/*.

179. Available from *www.timesonline.co.uk/tol/news/world/Afghanistan/article6811537.ece*.

180. Statement to the House of Commons by the Rt. Hon. Dr. John Reid, MP, January 26, 2006, available from *www.mod.uk/DefenceInternet/DefenceNews/MilitaryOperations/JohnReidbritishTaskForceHasAVitalJobToDoInSouthernAfghanistan.html*.

181. "UK Troops 'to target terrorists'," BBC News Website, April 24, 2006, available from *news.bbc.co.uk/2/hi/uk_news/4935532.stml*.

182. Indeed, Reid's quote formed the title for British journalist Christina Lamb's account of the Afghan War, "Not a Shot Fired," available from *bookshop.blackwell.co.uk/jsp/id/Not_A_Shot_Fired/9780007256921*.

183. Statement to the House of Commons by the Rt. Hon. Desmond Browne, MP, February 23, 2007, available from *www.guardian.co.uk/world/2007/feb/23/afghanistan.military*.

184. Richard Norton-Taylor, "UK's Afghan Mission at a Turning Point, says Browne," *Guardian*, August 16, 2007.

185. Statement to the House of Commons following the G8 by the Prime Minister Rt. Hon. Gordon Brown, MP, July 13, 2009.

186. Available from *www.timesonline.co.uk/tol/news/world/iraq/article6687944.ece.*

187. Available from *www.publications.parliament.uk/pa/cm200809/cmhansrd/cm090716/debtext/90716-0011.htm.*

188. Available from *www.publications.parliament.uk/pa/cm200809/cmhansrd/cm090716/debtext/90716-0012.htm.*

189. Available from *www.number10.gov.uk/Page20515.*

190. Cited in Volpe, p. 120.

191. Available from *nobelprize.org/nobel_prizes/peace/laureates/1957/pearson-bio.html.*

192. Gross-Stein, p. 196.

193. Pew Global Attitudes Survey, April 2004.

194. Philip Everts and Pierangelo Isernia, eds., *Public Opinion and the International Use of Force*, New York: Routledge, 2001, p. 238.

195. Volpe, p. 429.

196. "Alliance of the Unwilling," *Time International*, April 2008.

197. Available from *www.cbc.ca/news/america/finaldata.pdf.*

198. Ekos Research Associates Poll, February 2006, source *Angus Reid Global Monitor.*

199. Angus Reid Global Poll, July 2009, source *Angus Reid Global Monitor.*

200. Available from *ww.ctv.ca/servlet/ArticleNews/story/CTVNews/20060517/nato_afghan_060517/20060517?hub=CTVNewsAt11.*

201. Available from *www.cbc.ca/canada/story/2008/03/13/motion-confidence.html.*

202. Michael Ignatieff MP, Question Period, April 7, 2008.

203. Author's interview with Janice Gross-Stein, August 17, 2009.

204. Examples include Chris Wattie, *Contact Charlie: The Canadian Army, the Taliban and the Battle that saved Afghanistan*, Toronto, Canada: Key Porter Books, 2008; R. J. Hillier and Colonel Bernd Horn, *No Ordinary Men: Special Forces Missions in Afghanistan*, Toronto, Canada: Dundum Press, 2009; and Kevin Patterson and Jane Warren, *Outside the Wire: the War for Afghanistan in the Words of its Participants*, Toronto, Canada: Random House, 2007.

205. "Playing Politics with Afghanistan," Editorial, *Globe and Mail*, September 11, 2008.

206. Angus Reid Polls, April, May, and June 2007, source: *Angus Reid Global Monitor*.

207. David Ljungren, "NATO's Afghanistan Mission in Trouble: Canadian Senate," Reuters News Agency, February 12, 2007, available from *www.reuters.com/article/featuredCrisis/idUSN12426542.*

208. "Nicholas Sarkozy to bolster force in Afghanistan with 1,000 extra troops," *Times*, March 22, 2008; "The first Canadian poll taken after the French deployment showed support down by 8% to 33%," *Harris Decima*, August 2008.

209. Available from *www.thestrategiccounsel.com/our_news/polls/2006-08-14 GMCTV Aug 10-13 (Aug 14).pdf.*

210. Ekos Research Associates Poll, March 2006, source: *Angus Reid Global Monitor*.

211. June 6, 2006, Decima Research had 54 percent of Canadians opposed to the war, with 41 percent in favor; June 14, 2006, Strategic Counsel Poll had 48 percent in favor and 44 percent opposed. Source: *Angus Reid Global Monitor*.

212. Strategic Counsel Poll, September 2008, shows 61 percent opposition to the war.

213. The last poll showing majority support for the war in Canada is the Innovative Research Group's January 2007 poll which showed 58 percent support. Source: *Angus Reid Global Monitor*.

214. Gross-Stein, p. 243.

215. An IPSOS Reid poll shows majority support for the war in August 2007, but the general trend from January 2007 is for majority opposition. IPSOS Reid's poll is an outlier.

216. Gross-Stein, p. 287; David Ljungren, "NATO's Afghanistan Mission in Trouble: Canadian Senate," Reuters News Agency, February 12, 2007, available from *www.reuters.com/article/featuredCrisis/idUSN12426542*.

217. Available from *www.cbc.ca/news/background/afghanistan/casualties/list.html*.

218. Angus Reid Polls, February 20, 2007, 8 days after the report, asked if Canadian forces should be withdrawn before their mandate expired in February 2009. Only 41 percent disagreed. Compare with the Innovative Research Group's poll of the previous month which showed 58 percent in favor of Canadian troops being sent to Afghanistan. The questions are differently worded but are analytically the same.

219. Available from *icasualties.org/OEF/ByNationality.aspx*.

220. Gross-Stein, p. 199.

221. *Ibid.*, p. 196.

222. *Ibid.*, p. 210.

223. *Ibid.*, p. 239.

224. *Ibid.* p. 237.

225. Fareed Zakaria GPS, "Pakistani Government Achieves Truce with Taliban," Transcripts, March 1, 2009.

226. Angus Reid Strategies, September 2007.

227. Pew Global Attitudes Project, June 27, 2007.

228. Available from *www.washingtonpost.com/wp-dyn/articles/A60915-2004Nov18.html.*

229. Available from *kingsofwar.wordpress.com/2008/06/08/an-army-falling-apart/.*

230. Natalie La Balme, "The French and the Use of Force," in Everts and Isernia, p. 192.

231. *Ibid.*, pp. 189-191.

232. *Ibid.*, pp. 192, 196-197.

233. Available from *www.cbc.ca/news/america/finaldata.pdf.*

234. *Ibid.*

235. *Ibid.*

236. Pew Global Attitudes Project, "Global Public Opinion in the Bush Years (2001-2008)," December 18, 2008.

237. *Ibid.*

238. *Ibid.*

239. Available from *www.worldpublicopinion.org/pipa/articles/international_security_bt/535.php?lb=btot&pnt=535&nid=&id=.*

240. Available from *www.ambafrance-uk.org/French-presence-in-Afghanistan.html.*

241. "Alliance of the Unwilling," *Time International*, April 7, 2008.

242. Available from *abcnews.go.com/International/wireStory ?id=5531136.*

243. Available from *www.cnn.com/2008/WORLD/europe/03/26/ france.britain/index.html;* also available from *news.bbc.co.uk/2/hi/ europe/6630797.stm.*

244. Available from *www.telegraph.co.uk/news/worldnews/ asia/afghanistan/2585674/Taliban-kill-10-French-paratroopers-in-Afghanistan-ambush.html.*

245. Available from *uk.reuters.com/article/idUKL4116640 20080904.*

246. Available from *www.ambafrance-ca.org/spip.php?article 2404;* The French constitution reserves military and foreign affairs to the President, parliamentary approval is not usually required before deploying troops overseas.

247. Available from *icasualties.org/OEF/DeathsByYear.aspx.*

248. Available from *www.cnn.com/2009/WORLD/europe/03/11/ france.sarkozy.nato/index.html.*

249. Le Croix Poll, November 2001; Pew Global Attitudes Project, April 2002; BVA/L'Express Poll, September 2008.

250. Pew Global, June 27, 2007.

251. Available from *www.angus-reid.com/polls/view/french_ majority_opposes_role_in_afghanistan/.*

252. Available from *www.u-m-p.org/site/index.php/ump/l_ump/ notre_histoire.*

253. Available from *hebdo.parti-socialiste.fr/2008/04/02/1226/.*

254. *Ibid.*

255. La Balme, p. 191.

256. Available from *www.lemonde.fr/cgibin/ACHATS/acheter.cgi?offre=ARCHIVES&type_item=ART_ARCH_30J&objet_id=1000476.*

257. Available from *affaires-strategiques.iris-france.org/spip.php?article116.*

258. Available from *www.lepoint.fr/actualites-monde/2008-10-06/un-general-britannique-predit-un-echec-militaire-en-afghanistan/1648/0/279806.*

259. Available from *hebdo.parti-socialiste.fr/2008/04/02/1226/.*

260. Available from *www.ambafrance-uk.org/Joint-declaration-on-Afghanistan.html.*

261. Speech by Jacques Chirac, President of the French Republic, at the International Conference on Drug Routes, Paris, France, May 22, 2003.

262. "Chirac says France will keep troops in Afghanistan," Agence France Presse, October 2005.

263. Available from *www.montesquieu-institute.eu/9353000/1/j9vvhfxcd6p0lcl/vgnldm4wfwze?ctx=vg09llo6puxp.*

264. Available from *www.washingtonpost.com/wp-dyn/content/article/2007/04/18/AR2007041802245.html.*

265. Available from *www.nytimes.com/2008/06/30/world/europe/30iht-politicus.1.14095817.html.*

266. Available from *www.cfr.org/publication/13114/kupchan.html.*

267. Available from *www.spiegel.de/international/europe/0,1518,479838,00.html.*

268. Pew Global Attitudes Project, June 27, 2007; Angus Reid Polls, "French Oppose Commitments to Afgan Mission," April 18, 2008.

269. "Sarkozy resolute on Afghanistan despite the deaths of 10 French soldiers," *Christian Science Monitor*, August 20, 2008.

270. Available from *tempsreel.nouvelobs.com/depeches/politique/20080820.FAP1530/patrick_devedjian_critique_lattitude_du_ps_sur_lafghani.html.*

271. *Ibid.*

272. Available from *tempsreel.nouvelobs.com/actualites/politique/20080922.OBS2254/debat_sur_lafghanistan__le.* Translated from French by the author.

273. *Ibid.*

274. *Ibid.*

275. Angus Reid Polls, "French Oppose Commitments to Afgan Mission," April 18, 2008.

276. BVA/L'Express Poll, September 2008.

277. Ifop/Le Monde Poll, June 2008.

278. Available from *www.frontnational.com/communique_detail.php?id=1762.*

279. Available from *www.washingtonpost.com/wp-dyn/content/article/2007/04/13/AR2007041301401.html.*

280. Available from *tempsreel.nouvelobs.com/actualites/politique/20080922.OBS2254/debat_sur_lafghanistan__le.*

281. *Ibid.*

282. *Ibid.*

283. *Ibid.*

284. *Ibid.*

285. Anja Dalgaard-Nielsen, *Germany, Pacifism and Peace Enforcement*, Manchester, UK: Manchester University Press, 2006.

286. Everts and Isernia, pp. 254-255.

287. Dalgaard-Nielsen, pp. 70-71.

288. Everts and Isernia, pp. 72-72.

289. *Ibid.*, p. 73.

290. Pew Global Attitudes Project, June 27, 2007.

291. Pew Global Attitudes Project, "Global Public Opinion in the Bush Years (2001-2008)," December 18, 2009.

292. Available from *www.worldpublicopinion.org/pipa/articles/international_security_bt/535.php?lb=btot&pnt=535&nid=&id=*.

293. Available from *www.spiegelde/international/germany/0,1518,624880,00.html*.

294. Available from *www.dw-world.de/dw/article/0,,4000396,00.html*.

295. Available from *www.timesonline.co.uk/tol/news/world/europe/article6514742.ece*;*www.theaustralian.news.com.au/story/0,25197,25649897-31477,00.html*; also available from *atlanticreview.org/archives/1224-German-Soldiers-in-Afghanistan-Drinking-Instead-of-Fighting.html*; also available from *www.thesun.co.uk/sol/homepage/news/article577388.ece*.

296. Available from *www.weeklystandard.com/weblogs/TWSFP/2008/06/germany_to_send_1000_more_troo_1.asp*.

297. Gross-Stein, p. 202.

298. Available from *pewglobal.org/2002/04/17/americans-and-europeans-differ-widely-on-foreign-policy-issues/*.

299. *Ibid.*

300. Angus Reid Polls, "Pull Troops out of Afghanistan, Germans Say," March 21, 2007.

301. Angus Reid Polls, "Germans Would Remove Troops from Afghanistan," March 28, 2009.

302. Available from *icasualties.org/oef/byNationality.aspx?hnd Qry=Germany.*

303. *Ibid.*

304. That said, the lack of data for the period 2002-07 makes this conclusion only tentative. Polls taken especially in the wake of the successful suicide bombing on German ISAF troops in July 2003 would provide a powerful insight into the role of casualties in the trajectory of German support.

305. "Election Fears Said to Drive Merkel Policy on Afghanistan," *International Herald Tribune*, February 6, 2008.

306. Available from www.weeklystandard.com/Content/Public/Articles/000/000/014/211fkmyn.asp?pg=2.

307. Dalgaard-Nielsen, p. 86.

308. Available from *www.spiegel.de/international/germ ny/0,1518,472696,00.html.*

309. Available from *www.spiegel.de/international/world/0,1518,632535,00.html.*

310. Available from *www.zeit.de/online/2006/46/Afghanistan-Analyse.*

311. Available from *www.spiegel.de/politik/ausland/0,1518,445141,00.html.*

312. Available from *www.sueddeutsche.de/politik/277/417043/text/.*

313. Available from *www.berlinonline.de/berliner-zeitung/archiv/.bin/dump.fcgi/2007/1203/politik/0120/index.html.*

314. Available from *www.sueddeutsche.de/politik/437/425195/text/.*

315. Available from *www.focus.de/politik/ausland/afghanistan-einsatz_aid_56848.html.*

316. Available from *ipsnews.net/news.asp?idnews=38512.*

317. Available from *www.presseportal.de/pm/41150/1444504/die_linke.*

318. Available from *www.spiegel.de/international/germany/0,15 18,624880,00.html.*

319. Available from *www.spiegel.de/international/germany/0,1 518,472696,00.html.*

320. Available from *news.bbc.co.uk/2/hi/europe/1107628.stm.*

321. Paul Bermann, *Power and the Idealists: Or, the Passion of Joschka Fischer and Its Aftermath.* New York: Soft Skull Press, 2005.

322. Available from *www.gruene-bundestag.de/cms/bundestagsreden/dok/18/18471.joschka_fischer_afghanistaneinsatz.html.* Speech to the Bundestag by Joschka Fischer, 2005. Original in German, translation by the author.

323. Available from *www.auswaertiges-amt.de/diplo/de/Infoservice/Presse/Reden/Archiv/2002/021202-AfghanistanPetersberg.html.* Address to the Petersburg/Konigswater Conference, December 2002. Original in German, translation by the author.

324. Gerhard Schroeder, "Germany will share the burden in Iraq," *New York Times,* September 2003.

325. Available from *www.spiegel.de/international/germany/0,15 18,630090,00.html.*

326. Available from *www.weeklystandard.com/Content/Public/Articles/000/000/014/211fkmyn.asp?pg=2.*

327. Available from *www.reuters.com/article/asiaCrisis/idUSL 231001602.*

328. Available from *www.auswaertiges-amt.de/diplo/en/Infoservice/Presse/Reden/2008/081007-Rede-BM-Afg-ISAF-BT.html.*

329. Dalgaard-Nielsen, p. 47.

330. Available from *www.nytimes.com/2001/11/17/world/pressing-greens-german-leader-wins-historic-vote-sending-troops-afghanistan.html.*

331. Available from *www.eurasianet.org/departments/insight/articles/eav101708a.shtml.*

332. Available from *www.telegraph.co.uk/news/worldnews/europe/germany/6237753/Guido-Westerwelle-profile-FDP-leader.html.*

333. Available from *www.spiegelde/international/germany/0,1518,623709,00.html.*

334. Available from *www.washingtonpost.com/wp-dyn/content/article/2009/09/08/AR2009090800715.html.*

335. Angus Reid Polls, "Germans Mount Pressure on Afghan Withdrawl," December 6, 2009.

336. Alexander L. George, and Andrew Bennett, *Case Studies and Theory Development in the Social Sciences*, Cambridge, MA: MIT Press, 2005, p. 161.

337. *Ibid.*, p. 165.

U.S. ARMY WAR COLLEGE

Major General Robert M. Williams
Commandant

*****

STRATEGIC STUDIES INSTITUTE

Director
Professor Douglas C. Lovelace, Jr.

Director of Research
Dr. Antulio J. Echevarria II

Author
Mr. Charles A. Miller

Director of Publications
Dr. James G. Pierce

Publications Assistant
Ms. Rita A. Rummel

*****

Composition
Mrs. Jennifer E. Nevil

Lightning Source UK Ltd.
Milton Keynes UK
UKOW07f2008220615

253950UK00010B/352/P